**Praise for *The Sales L***

"What Suzanne Paling does in *The Sales Leader's Problem Solver* is provide a step-by-step process for how to attack the myriad of unique management issues faced by sales management. As a sales manager I would keep this book close by as a reference and starting point whenever a sales management issue was recognized."

—Pat Pallentino, director, FSU Sales Institute,
Sam Walton Fellow, Florida State University

"This book is both comprehensive and pragmatic. Suzanne's approach and content is relevant, and her examples are real-world. This would be a great tool for virtually anyone in sales management."

—Robert Nadeau, director, Professional Sales Program,
Plymouth State University

"Selling sales managers can play a critical role in small, but developing sales organizations. There were several great tips within this book about who best to put in the role, how important setting the right expectations are, and how to develop their sales management skills for success."

—Johanna Rivard, executive vice president, Pure B2B

"I couldn't agree more that a Selling Manager role is at best a very challenging approach and at worst a costly endeavor. Suzanne offers valuable advice on how to successfully establish and manage the Selling Manager."

—Steve Gunderson, principal, Transitional Data Services

"Recognizing sales problems is easy. Knowing how to address and solve for them is where every sales manager earns their keep. This book pragmatically addresses several sales challenges in ways that are easy to understand and execute on."

—Johanna Rivard, executive vice president, Pure B2B

"Suzanne Paling has presented a number of real world examples of sales and sales management problems and followed them up with realistic, common sense solutions. These solutions addresses both qualitatively and quantitatively the different elements of each challenge typically experienced by both sales and sales management."
—Mike Waldron, director, Enterprise Sales, Xactly Corporation

"Each chapter takes an in-depth look at difficult, yet often too common, situations a sales manager will face. Clear and actionable step-by-step instructions provide everything a sales manager needs for creating, communicating, implementing and documenting a measurable plan. At the end of each chapter you're reminded of your most important job as a sales manager - hiring the right people for the right job!"
—Brian Donovan, North America sales trainer, HomeAway

"*The Sales Leader's Problem Solver* provides sales managers with a targeted and essential resource for recognizing and handling situations faced by all sales managers. Suzanne provides a step-by-step guide to properly diagnose each situation and actionable advice with detailed instructions for sales leaders. This book helps to remove some of the mystery around managing a sales force and provides a playbook required to address critical situations that frequently derail the most seasoned sales teams."
—Frank Costanzo, senior vice president sales and business development, Caliper

SUZANNE M. PALING

# THE
# SALES
# LEADER'S
# PROBLEM
# SOLVER

Practical Solutions to
Conquer Management Mess-Ups,
Handle Difficult Sales Reps,
and Make the Most of Every Opportunity

CAREER
PRESS
Wayne, N.J.

THE SALES LEADER'S PROBLEM SOLVER
EDITED BY ROGER SHEETY
TYPESET BY KARA KUMPEL
Cover design by Rob Johnson/Toprotype
Cube image by ip studio/shutterstock
Printed in the U.S.A.

To order this title, please call toll-free 1-800-CAREER-1 (NJ and Canada: 201-848-0310) to order using VISA or MasterCard, or for further information on books from Career Press.

CAREER PRESS

The Career Press, Inc.
12 Parish Drive
Wayne, NJ 07470
www.careerpress.com

Library of Congress Cataloging-in-Publication Data
CIP Data Available Upon Request.

Robert F. Paling

1929–2011

We all miss you, Dad.

Jim

Thanks again for all your help.

# Acknowledgments

Thank you to the following people for their generous assistance in the pre-publication effort: Jill Konrath of Jill Konrath, Inc., John Willig of Literary Services, Inc., Lori Richardson of Score More Sales, and Robert Holland, PhD, of Vistage Michigan.

For their help in providing valuable information for the book, I would like to express my gratitude to David Sawyer of Safer Places, Bob Perkins and Brooke Niesen of the AA-ISP, and Sherry Acque and Frank Costanzo of Caliper.

Finally, I appreciate all the efforts on my behalf from the entire Career Press team.

# Contents

# Foreword

In this book, *The Sales Leader's Problem Solver*, Suzanne Paling identifies 15 perplexing problems that sales leaders continually confront, but seldom successfully solve. She shows how to accurately identify the problem, find its multiple causes, and drill down into alternative solutions. This book is a pleasant read and there are no wasted words. Each chapter starts with a vignette to illustrate the problem, then the necessary data to identify its possible causes, and examples of meaningful dialogues with salespeople that will successfully solve the problem. Solutions from these meaningful dialogues vary from better hiring and training practices to changing compensation incentives to changing sales force organization.

As a sales leader your job is to make the salespeople successful, but there are common road blocks, such as bad salesperson and sales manager habits, which prevent that. Suzanne provides practical, step-by-step methods to successfully remove these road blocks and correct the bad habits. The methods are based on her many years of experience as a sales management consultant. Each chapter contains checklists, templates, worksheets, and narratives custom designed to help you navigate these situations.

Sales drive profits and good sales management drive sales. Good sales management properly applied is the least expensive and most effective way to increase revenues, market share, margins, cash flow, and ROI. The book deals with "growth busters," frequent frustrating problems that sales leaders have to deal with. You will meet sales reps you all know. The book saves you time and money by giving you a proven hands-on formula for dealing with these common problems.

Your job as a sales leader is to get work done through other people, your sales team, but when they are prevented from being successful by common problems, you need a guide on how to turn the problem into an opportunity. Each chapter of *The Sales Leader's Problem Solver* deals with proven step-by-step ways to deal with one of these common challenges.

The solutions to these 15 major sales leader's problems are broken into bite-sized pieces that are easy to apply from a list of "do's and don'ts." If a particular solution is not effective, suggestions are made on alternative courses of action. The book shows that sales force management is a process and that one step logically follows another. Control the pieces and you control the whole.

The audience for this book includes those directly managing salespeople and those responsible for the sales managers. The audience should also include those salespeople on a career path to management. Understanding the problems addressed in each chapter will help the newly promoted sales manager anticipate the challenges ahead.

The book will help any sales leader successfully manage a variety of salespeople, including new hires and veterans. It will help with not only understanding these 15 common problems and their possible causes, but also how to execute and implement the solutions. It will help sales leaders to manage a changing landscape.

Successful sales leaders understand their job is to get work done through other people and this book will help them do that.

Robert J. Calvin

Author of *Sales Management Demystified*, McGraw-Hill;

*Sales Management*, The McGraw-Hill Executive MBA Series;

*Entrepreneurial Management*, The McGraw-Hill Executive MBA Series

previously adjunct professor, sales management and entrepreneurship, University of Chicago, Booth School of Business

# Introduction

Rene worked for five years as a sales rep with her current employer. A career salesperson with 10 years' experience, Rene considered herself a solid performer, always making or exceeding quota.

When her manager resigned, Rene approached company president Don about the job. After several meetings between the two, Don offered Rene the position—her first as a sales manager.

Newly hired sales reps at the company were immediately enrolled in a sales training program. Rene had taken the course and benefitted substantially. She approached Don about attending the sales management course and was shocked when he turned her down. The price, commensurate with what the company spent on sales training, was "not in the budget."

Wanting to interact with and learn from peers, Rene put in a request to join the local Sales Management Association at $600 per year. That request was denied too. Regrouping, Rene asked Don to send her to "Tips for New Managers" for $129. He grudgingly agreed to let her spend a day out of the office. Sitting in a large hotel conference room with 300 other new managers, Rene picked up several helpful tips, but none related specifically to sales management.

Don's attitude confused and angered Rene. He spent money training reps (many of whom didn't work out). For a sales manager with a quota responsibility of $23 million, he wouldn't make the investment.

Undaunted, Rene dove into the job with boundless energy. She read several books on sales management and put a lot of thought into how to structure the job. Early initiatives included: scheduling weekly one-on-one meetings with each rep, accompanying them on sales calls, creating a sales contest, and redesigning the CRM (customer relationship management) dashboard.

As the newness of the position began to wear off, Rene took stock of the situation. Although she'd made well-received changes, she felt unsure of herself—especially when dealing with problematic situations. One of the reps rarely entered information in the CRM. Another never prospected for new business.

Rene knew both of these issues—and others—needed addressing. She just didn't know how to go about it. She longed for a 1-800 sales management hotline with a coach to walk her through the proper steps. She's trying hard and doing the best she can. That had to be enough for now.

***

So the story goes for the vast majority of professional sales managers. They watch rep after rep go through training, while little or no money gets budgeted for *their* professional development. They learn, largely on their own, to run a sales force.

Rene has the skills, interest, and temperament to succeed as a sales manager. She enjoys the requirements of the job such as:

- Reviewing sales forecasts.
- Analyzing and acting on data.
- Mentoring, motivating, and coaching.

- Recognizing and rewarding reps.
- Accompanying reps on sales calls.
- Recruiting and onboarding new sales hires.

Without proper training or peers to bounce ideas off of, she will
- Make unnecessary mistakes.
- Struggle to develop her style.
- Put in long hours.
- Miss revenue goals.
- Lack the knowledge to be a top performing manager.
- Look for another position offering training and support.

*The Sales Leader's Problem Solver* deconstructs and offers real world, step-by-step solutions for solving the most common difficulties and dilemmas sales managers face, such as:
- Approaching the rep.
- Structuring the discussion.
- Including management and human resources.
- Initiating disciplinary action if necessary.
- Setting policy to deal with future occurrences.
- Communicating with other staff members.

Though not all of the following points are applicable in every chapter, the potential solution(s) to the problems follow a similar structure:
- Vignette
- Problem summary
- Getting started
- Create a plan
- Present the plan to executives
- Address the issue with the rep
- Current staff
- Hiring
- New hire orientation
- Leadership opportunities
- Summary checklist
- Resolution

# Vignette

Each chapter begins with a short story describing an issue facing a sales leader. The narratives come directly from my experience as a corporate sales manager and more than 15 years as a sales management consultant.

These vignettes establish common ground. Many readers of my previous book, *The Accidental Sales Manager*, said they "recognized themselves or others in these stories." The reader's reaction, "I'm not the only one facing this problem," opens the door for outlining the issue and beginning to address it.

# Problem summary

Confused, angry, and frustrated sales managers frequently react emotionally to a problem:

- How could this have happened?
- I bet other sales managers don't deal with this.
- Part of the blame falls on the marketing department, but they won't be brought to task.
- I'm stumped as to how to fix this issue.
- I'll look really bad if I don't solve this problem.
- I wish I had someone to talk to about this.

The summary offers a simple and objective outline of the issue, giving beleaguered sales leaders a chance to focus, center themselves, and face the problem with objectivity.

# Getting started

"I can't stand by and ignore this situation any longer. But what do I do first? Talk to a colleague, my boss, the rep? Should I put the salesperson on probation?" asks the sales leader. Taking that initial step often causes the most anxiety.

Sharing the problem with someone (anyone) might make them feel better, but only temporarily. Often it's the *worst* first step. In this section, sales leaders get *specific* advice on what to do first. I advise researching the issue, and gathering data to put together a fact-based approach to solving the problem.

When they are ready to discuss the problem with others, sales managers following this guidance talk about the situation less emotionally and are better prepared.

## Create a plan

Frustrated sales executives often say, "I broached the topic of solving this problem during our monthly one-on-one. I got shot down immediately." Others tell stories of discussing potential solutions to a difficult situation at a business lunch only to have the president quickly dismiss the subject. This makes them hesitant to try again.

Rather than bringing the subject up a second or third time, I advise sales managers to use the information from their research to put a report together with a suggested plan. Most question this suggestion initially. "If he dismissed it at lunch, why would he read a report?"

Crafting a plan shows commitment. It allows sales executives to include facts, figures, and examples to bolster their case. Company leaders read, review, and consider the proposal at their convenience. They respect the effort put in by the sales executive. This leads to a more balanced and serious discussion of the matter.

## Present the plan to executives

Sales leaders often operate without allies on an executive team. Some find themselves at odds with marketing, finance, or product development. Sales executives usually have one of the highest profile jobs within the company. When their team achieves quota, their hero status doesn't always sit well with other executives. If they come in under quota, sometimes their fellow managers gloat.

Because of this dynamic, sales leaders often feel obliged to handle *any* difficulties within the sales organization *on their own*. They worry about the message it sends if they reach out for assistance. This kind of thinking makes asking for help all the more difficult.

Those leading the sales force benefit from understanding how to enlist the CEO's help, anticipate pitfalls, defend themselves against, and gain support from, their fellow managers.

## Address the issue with the rep

Most leaders know *exactly* what they want to say to the salesperson in question. They often fumble with choosing the right words to get the conversation *started*. This hesitation leads to rambling, accusatory, or vague discussions.

I provide one or two scripts with precise wording to begin the talk. These words and phrases leave no room for doubt about the issue being discussed. But the rep doesn't feel criticized or immediately put on the defensive. This leads to targeted and productive discussions.

## Current staff

"During our last staff meeting, I had a serious talk with my team. They know where I stand, and promised to improve," sales managers all over the country say with grave sincerity. And they mean it. And the reps do improve—for a period of time.

Then managers get busy with an important deal—hiring for an empty territory needs to happen right way, a crisis occurs with an important customer, and so on—until several months have gone by. Managers stop paying attention and the reps go back to their old ways.

Managers get advice for dealing with each rep one-on-one, tailoring the discussion to *individual* performance issues, following up, following through, not getting sidetracked, and continuing to monitor the situation.

## Hiring

Many difficulties with reps originate with the interview process: questions go unasked, some topics get glossed over, and key employees miss out on the opportunity to speak with the candidate.

Sales managers receive guidance on asking *specific* questions to minimize the chances of the particular problem occurring with the new hire. This ensures new salespeople begin their employment with a better understanding of company expectations around their performance.

## New hire orientation

Busy sales leaders sometimes hasten or forgo a thorough orientation process. Others avoid any discussion of difficult subjects in the early weeks, wanting new hires to enjoy a "honeymoon" period.

New hire orientation provides the ideal platform for reinforcing subjects of importance covered during the interview process. Sales leaders need to make sure that certain topics get covered in a positive way during this time.

## Leadership opportunities

Though it doesn't always seem like it at the time, any issue, problem, or dilemma represents a leadership opportunity. Rather than shy away from it, sales leaders need to face these situations head-on.

Successfully dealing with a troublesome issue enhances the reputation and career of a sales leader resolving the difficulty in a positive manner.

## Summary checklist

Before calling a project complete, managers need a checklist. Like the issue outlined in the beginning of each chapter, this allows them to revisit the problem unemotionally. The to-do list holds sales leaders accountable to those last few details so they don't rush to prematurely call the issue solved.

## Resolution

Each chapter concludes with a vignette letting the reader know how the problem was resolved.

## In conclusion

Those managing salespeople have a variety of titles: sales manager, director of sales, or vice president of sales. Some supervise two reps in a small division. Others have many more reps reporting directly to them. The sales staff might consist of field, inside, or remote reps—or a combination of all three. Some reps work in foreign countries.

Regardless of the size of your team, the industry you work in, your years of experience, or your level of seniority, all sales leaders face problems. Not every sales leader has or ever will have every difficulty in this book. But many will have to confront at least a few at some point in their career.

The good news is that with some planning, patience, and effort, solutions to these problems exist—and you can be the one to solve them. Don't spend another day feeling helpless or ineffective. Read the chapter, follow the instructions, add your own ideas, and get the problem solved. You can do it.

# Chapter 1
# The Inconsistent Sales Rep

Looking over the numbers for February, sales manager Kyle sees that Stan exceeded his quota by 30 percent. Kyle wants to jump for joy. He used to; he knows better now. In March, Stan will just miss his goal, and then be off by 20 percent in April. He'll squeak by in June, while playing the role of hero in July, exceeding quota by 25 percent. And on and on it will go, month after month, quarter after quarter, all year long.

Discussions with Stan about his up and down, roller coaster-like performance prove fruitless. A friendly likeable guy, he puts Kyle's suggestions to use almost immediately. A few weeks later he stops. Kyle then questions why he bothered.

Later that day he meets with Maria to talk about her uncharacteristically low February numbers. She looks at him and says, "I know. I really 'pulled a Stan' didn't I?" Kyle realizes Stan's erratic numbers have become a staff joke. As the leader, he knows this makes him look bad, too.

Given his erratic performance, Stan either just makes or just misses his annual sales number—every year. Kyle sticks with him because when he's on, he's on. He comes through sometimes like no other rep. Kyle wishes he knew how to handle this situation.

---

### Problem summary

Sales rep

- Achieves quota inconsistently
- Occasionally closes a record number of sales to save the month or quarter
- Affects team morale and income with erratic performances

Sales manager

- Cannot count on the rep to achieve quota
- Wastes time speaking to and coaching the rep
- Knows sales staff thinks he enables the behavior

---

Companies depend on salespeople achieving quota. When this doesn't happen, cash flow problems, terminations, layoffs, and outright business failures take place. Organizations hire sales executives to guide this effort.

Sales executives tolerating an inconsistent sales performance unwittingly sanction this behavior. It calls into question their ability to lead their group. The situation has to be brought under control.

## Getting started

Minimize feelings of frustration with the rep by gathering and analyzing the facts. Identify cycles and patterns. Run the numbers in different ways to determine this rep's:

- Monthly average.
- Seasonal highs or lows.
- Highest and lowest revenue months.
- Months of missed quota.
- Strongest and weakest product area.

The following chart compares the reps' annual sales results (monthly quota $90,000).

| | January | February | March | April | May | June | July | August |
|---|---|---|---|---|---|---|---|---|
| Cathy | $107,000 | $104,500 | $101,200 | $97,700 | $99,200 | $109,000 | $98,300 | $122,600 |
| Jed | $84,000 | $88,200 | $104,800 | $101,700 | $107,900 | $98,400 | $99,170 | $100,005 |
| Stan | $109,500 | $117,030 | $91,030 | $65,700 | $73,000 | $66,400 | $81,000 | $94,300 |
| Maria | $95,000 | $89,000 | $92,900 | $105,100 | $91,000 | $93,500 | $96,900 | $90,005 |

| September | October | November | December | Total | Quota | % of Quota | Difference |
|---|---|---|---|---|---|---|---|
| $103,700 | $102,900 | $108,100 | $110,000 | $1,264,200 | $1,080,000 | 117% | $184,200 |
| $106,900 | $100,400 | $104,300 | $103,800 | $1,199,575 | $1,080,000 | 111% | $119,575 |
| $124,000 | $105,700 | $4,200 | $82,200 | $1,084,060 | $1,080,000 | 100% | $4,060 |
| $92,000 | $93,200 | $91,000 | $95,000 | $1,124,605 | $1,080,000 | 104% | $44,605 |

Missed Quota

A manager looking at these numbers sees that Jed struggled early in the year. He recovered and exceeded quota since then. Maria missed her February goal. Though never a top producer, her sales remain steady.

Stan reaches a high of $117,030 in February, just hits quota in March, and then misses quota for four consecutive months. His sales climb back up in August, reach a high in September, and drop in October. He misses quota in November and December.

The following chart compares the reps' monthly average:

| Rep | Total | Mo. Avg. |
| --- | --- | --- |
| Cathy | $ 1,264,200 | $ 105,350 |
| Jed | $ 1,199,575 | $ 99,965 |
| Stan | $ 1,084,060 | $ 90,338 |
| Maria | $ 1,123,705 | $ 93,642 |

Maria reached a high in July ($96,900) versus Stan ($124,000) in September. Yet she outsells him by $3,000 for the year. His low months affect his annual performance.

After reviewing the data further, a manager might realize this rep:

- Goes from a high to a medium to a low month.
- Experiences trouble recovering from a low month.
- Underperforms several months in a row.

The manager wants to shout, "Come into my office. I've solved the problem. Now I know why you have good and bad months. Here. Look at the numbers. We can stop this!! Don't let a shaky start to the month get you down. If you stay positive, you'll hit the goal!"

Keep the celebration on hold. The manager uncovered *a pattern*. He doesn't yet understand the *problem* nor have a *solution*.

## Create a plan

If a rep cycles between achieving and missing quota without facing any consequences, a policy gap may be to blame. No mechanism exists for dealing with the problem.

Start addressing the situation through modifications to the sales policy manual. Consider potential wording such as:

*Sales representatives failing to achieve quota for two consecutive months will be placed on probation. Those reps falling to achieve quota for a third month must meet with their manager to determine the next course of action—up to and including termination.*

Salespeople sometimes just make or miss a quota, whereas the other reps exceed their goal comfortably. Hold reps accountable when their monthly average falls below the group's average:

*Sales representatives falling below the group average for two consecutive months will be placed on probation. If a rep falls below the group average for a third month, they must meet with their manager to determine the next course of action—up to and including termination.*

Conceivably a rep could miss quota for two consecutive months, achieve quota the next, then miss for another two months running. Avoid this management energy drain through the following:

*Should a sales representative fall below the group average or fail to achieve quota for two consecutive months, twice in the same business year, they will be subject to termination.*

> Quick tip: When considering a change to the sales policy and procedures manual, take the opportunity to revisit the entire document. Make additional updates or revisions as needed. Doing so lessens the focus on the inconsistent performer on staff.

## Present the plan to executives

Review the charts and graphs with your direct supervisor. Discuss the findings. Present suggested sales policy manual additions or alterations for their approval. Be prepared to offer potential solutions for this particular problem.

Most company leaders, in my experience, make interesting and accurate observations about people. Removed from the day-to-day managing of the sales reps, they view things differently. Take advantage of this and benefit from their input and guidance. Listen to what they have to say. They may point out a few things you didn't think of.

## Address the issue with the rep

Not all "up and down" reps struggle in the same way. This problem shows up in *different* patterns, including:

- The "closing frenzy" rep: lackluster sales during the first few weeks of the month, followed by a rush to close deals during the last week.
- The "fading" rep: solid sales during the first two weeks of the month that dwindle during the last two weeks.
- The "collapsing" rep: three strong weeks of monthly sales, followed by a week of poor sales.

Each scenario leads to the same issue: unpredictable, roller coaster months or quarters. Understand the specific pattern before meeting one-on-one with the rep.

## Best time to talk

Maximize the effectiveness of the conversation by initiating the discussions during an "up" period for the reps:

- The "closing frenzy" rep: Begin a discussion toward the end of the month—just after they've closed a few sales.
- The "fading" or "collapsing" rep: Speak with him or her after the second strong week of sales.

Approaching reps during "up" not "down" times gives you the chance to talk to them when they're less frantic.

## Get clarity

Before scheduling any one-on-one meetings with this rep, be certain as sales leader that you know what these meetings are and are not about. These conferences focus on inconsistent sales performance and nothing else. No *sales skills* coaching should be discussed.

Reps like this already know how to prospect, assess needs, address objections, make presentations, and close deals. They've proven themselves many times.

## Begin the discussions

Say something like, "We've spoken before about your inconsistent sales performance. Looking at your sales figures, I made some interesting observations. Let me show you."

Give reps a chance to look at the data. Don't rush or push them into "seeing" a pattern. Just let them look at the graphs and charts. Allow the discussion to unfold.

## Use visuals

As a sales manager, I show reps data and comparative numbers all the time. Whenever I present the same information in graph form, attentiveness increases. Easier to read and often more dramatic, graphs drive the point home that much more effectively.

This shows the numbers from Table 1.1. You really feel and experience the roller coaster ride of the "up and down" rep.

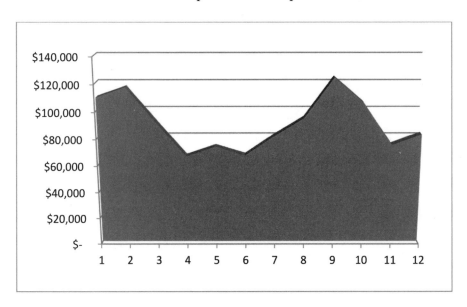

Close the initial conversation by saying something like, "For now, I'd appreciate you keeping our talk between the two of us. Look the information over. Let's meet in another day or two and discuss your observations."

Schedule another meeting or conference call there and then.

# Follow-up

During the second discussion, ask questions:

- What were you overall thoughts?
- What did you notice about your own performance?
- How did the other reps' performances compare to your own?
- Which data surprised you?

Keep the questions open-ended whenever possible. See what they have to say. During a second meeting, if they don't notice a pattern, point it out. Don't waste time.

The swinging pendulum sales performance detrimentally affects:

- Valuable management and coaching time.
- Predictability of the sales forecasts.
- Ability to achieve quarterly and year-end sales goals.
- The reps' income.

Though it may take a series of meetings to fully deal with this issue, state the obvious early on. Have reps leave this second meeting understanding that achieving quota, then missing for several months in a row has to stop.

# Future meetings

In this chapter, the sales manager realizes the rep experiences difficulty recovering from a slow week or month. Another rep with "up and down" sales might have a different pattern with the same frustrating results:

## Scenario #1

A rep with lackluster sales during the first one or two weeks of the month might be burned-out from rushing to close sales during the previous month.

## Scenario #2

A rep with strong sales during the first few weeks of the month could relax during the next two, assuming the sales will happen naturally.

## Scenario #3

Reps sputtering out during the last week might be guilty of overestimating how far along they were in the sales process with some of the prospects.

## Scenario #4

Many "up and down" reps suffer from pipeline mismanagement—never having enough potential deals in the earlier stages to close the required number of sales each month.

# Put the issue in writing

At this point, managers put something in writing, summarizing any discussions and outlining a game plan. Change things up. Ask the *rep* to put a plan in writing as in the following example:

---

To:        (Sales Executive)

From:     (Salesperson)

Date:      March 10, 2xxx

Re:        Performance against quota

-----------------------------------------------------------------------------

For the last several weeks [name of sales executive] and I have been discussing my inconsistent sales performance. I understand the impact it has on the whole company. To work on meeting and exceeding my goals, I agree to do the following:

- Schedule a meeting with my sales manager if I meet less than 15 percent of my monthly total in the first week
- Interact regularly with the steadier producers
- Ask for, listen to, and act on their advice
- Increase all sales related activities (prospecting, demonstrations, proposals) by a minimum of 20 percent during lighter months
- Read and discuss [name of book] with the sales manager

---

> • Refuse to give up on the month if the first few weeks are slow
>
> _____
> Salesperson
> Company X
>
> _____
> Sales Executive
> Company X

Taking the extra step of creating a contract adds a certain gravitas as well as underscoring the salesperson's responsibilities and obligations.

## Current staff

Understandably frustrated with the "up and down" situation, a manager might be tempted to write a new sales policy and hand it out at a staff meeting with little explanation. Several months later, when the rep in question fails to achieve quota two months in a row, the manager could:

- Put him on probation.
- Eventually terminate his employment.
- Consider the problem solved.

That behavior looks angry and punitive. Instead, in a predicament like this, work with reps in this situation for a reasonable period of time. Give them a fair chance to improve the erratic sales performance, and then discuss policy changes with the sales team.

During the end of a regular staff meeting, say something like:

"All organizations revisit policies and procedures. The president and I reviewed several current sales policies and made a few revisions. Specifically, we made changes to [give examples]. Please read it over. I'll be discussing this with you and answering questions during our one-on-ones later today and tomorrow."

## One-on-one meetings

During these talks, never discuss a specific salesperson. Mention, instead, noticing a *trend* of inconsistent sales months among the staff. Talk about the difficulties this causes and your desire to solve the problem. Answer any questions. Listen to their views.

If reps voice serious objections to the new policy, hear them out. If one of them makes a great suggestion, take notes about the particulars and discuss it with your boss. Get back to them, but tell them the policy stands for the foreseeable future. After a period of time, you'll be open to discussing potential adjustments.

# Hiring

Include questions about consistency during in-person interviews such as:

- In which months/quarters did you sell the most this year?
- In which months/quarters did you sell the least?
- Any particular reason why?
- In your sales career, have there been particular months or quarters that have always been strong for you?
- Have any months been historically lower?

Through this line of questioning, detect any patterns if possible.

# New hire orientation

Recent hires get the lay of the land fairly quickly. They see one or more reps hit their quota intermittently. This leads them to believe that this behavior is okay. Why would they think any differently? No one gets terminated because of it.

Discuss sales department policies and procedures during the later stages of the interview process. Reinforce the policies during their first 90 days with your organization. Look for "up and down" sales months. If it occurs, address it early on. Going forward, new hires need to understand that inconsistent sales performances have consequences.

# Leadership opportunities

Leaders know salespeople influence one another. Selling alongside high performing reps motivates a rep to work harder and exceed their own goals.

Unfortunately, this works both ways. Allowing one rep to perform inconsistently with no penalties opens the door for other reps to follow suit. During a slow month or quarter, they might give up instead of pushing through.

Failure to address this issue allows an "up and down" rep to unduly influence the group. It calls your ability to lead into question.

# Summary checklist
## Inconsistent rep review and checklist

- Clarify problem.
- Review monthly productivity reports.
- Determine patterns:
  - Several low sales months in a row.
  - Strong sales during the first few weeks of the month followed by slow sales.
  - Slow sales during the early weeks followed by a closing frenzy.
- Involve direct supervisor.
- Retool:
  - Policies and procedures.
  - Minimum performance standards.
- Speak with "up and down" rep.
- Collaborate on solving the issue.
- Address current staff.
- Hold inconsistent rep(s) accountable.

# Resolution

At week's end, Stan achieved only 10 percent of his monthly number. In keeping with their agreement (sales during the first week of the month of less than 15 percent of total goal), he sets up a meeting with Kyle.

Kyle knows nothing motivates Stan like talking about exceeding quota, as he did last month. So during their meeting he asks him, "What went on last month?" Stan's energy changes as he reminisces about successful appointments and signed contracts.

Stan will never be Kyle's most consistent performer. He missed quota twice during the past seven months. The difference is he didn't miss quota two months in a row. That's a huge improvement. Kyle has succeeded in his objective of stopping Stan's 2–4 months downward slide.

With the sales staff, Kyle notices Stan gets more respect. He's glad to see this. In addition, Stan receives larger and more consistent commission checks. This has contributed to his having a more even demeanor with customers.

Once he'd uncovered Stan's erratic sales cycle, Kyle noticed other reps' patterns. For instance, Maria's strongest sales occur during the second week of the month—for productivity standards as well as sales. Always.

Can she apply some of what happens during that week to a few of the other weeks? If so, she could increase her income. He'll discuss this with her during week three. She's always in a great mood after a strong second week.

# Chapter 2
# Selling Only to Existing Customers

Laura has no peer when it comes to increasing business with existing customers. She maximizes opportunities within a department. In turn, those department leaders introduce her to decision-makers throughout the company. Because of this ability, she's realized double-digit growth in previously stagnant accounts.

The problem: in three years with the company she has yet to open one new account.

Laura leaves notes In the CRM system about "stopping in to see" potential clients. Ellen, director of sales, reviews those account records and sees no mention of follow-up meetings. Furthermore, Laura routinely ignores the qualified leads she receives.

During quarterly reviews with Ellen, Laura amiably agrees to prospect and follow up on leads. But she doesn't. Recently, the competition signed a three-year contract at a well-known firm in Laura's territory. She has never called on this company.

Laura's talent with existing clients always stops Ellen from holding her accountable for the lack of new ones. But she needs Laura to mine that territory for new business. Ellen realizes she has to do something.

---

### Problem summary

Sales rep

- Makes half-hearted efforts at cold calling
- Fails to follow up with potential new clients
- Schedules no meetings with key companies in her territory
- Closes no new business

Company president

- Values the rep's ability with existing customers
- Hesitates to hold the rep accountable for cold calling
- Watches competition close deals in the rep's territory

---

Within any company's roster of clients, natural attrition takes place. A percentage of customers go out of business, switch vendors, or change corporate direction. For a company to grow, sales reps must bring in new business.

# Getting started

This rep brings in *no new business whatsoever*. As a first step, look at new business productivity for the entire sales staff to determine:

- Total new business revenue.
- Top new business producer.
- New business revenue by quarter or annually.

| | Q1 | Q2 | Q3 | Q4 | Total | Average |
|---|---|---|---|---|---|---|
| Brad | $ 17,000 | $ 5,000 | $ 20,700 | $ 9,000 | $ 51,700 | $ 12,925 |
| Jean | $ 100,000 | $ 80,000 | $ 40,000 | $ 75,000 | $ 295,000 | $ 73,750 |
| Laura | $ - | $ - | $ - | $ - | $ - | $ - |
| Darren | $ 63,000 | $ 57,000 | $ 44,000 | $ 79,800 | $ 243,800 | $ 60,950 |
| Connie | $ 32,000 | $ 18,000 | $ 34,000 | $ 26,000 | $ 110,000 | $ 27,500 |
| Total | $ 212,000 | $ 160,000 | $ 138,700 | $ 189,800 | $ 700,500 | $ 175,125 |

Analyze new business as a percentage of quota:

| | New Business | Quota | Percentage |
|---|---|---|---|
| Brad | $ 51,700 | $ 1,900,000 | 2.7% |
| Jean | $ 295,000 | $ 2,100,000 | 14.0% |
| Laura | $ - | $ 2,000,000 | 0.0% |
| Darren | $ 243,800 | $ 2,200,000 | 11.1% |
| Connie | $ 110,000 | $ 2,100,000 | 5.2% |
| Totals | $ 700,500 | $ 10,300,000 | 6.8% |

Jean and Darren lead the group in new business revenue and as a percentage of their quota. Although Brad and Connie bring in some new business, their productivity needs addressing. Now you see the new business performance of the staff as a whole.

# Create a plan

Solving this problem involves reviewing:

- Sales skills.
- Minimum performance standards.
- Compensation.
- Policy and procedure.

# Sales skills

Reps excelling at managing and increasing business within an *existing* account aren't necessarily talented prospectors. Successful cold callers possess certain sales skill sets like getting through to decision-makers and bouncing back from rejection.

Before investing management/coaching time with this or any other rep you manage, make sure they have the traits and skills necessary to find and close new business. Have each rep take an online sales assessment.

If assessment results show one or more reps need help with prospecting, your company needs to invest in sales training.

> Quick tip: By assessing the entire group, a sales leader avoids isolating or calling attention to the underperforming rep. Assessments point out strengths and weaknesses. The focus moves to improving the prospecting abilities of the entire sales staff.

# Setting minimum performance standards

Though sales leaders *talk about* new business, many stop short of making it a requirement of the job. Those serious about generating new business revenue set minimum performance standards for prospecting. They establish specific goals around behavior and action.

# Prospecting activity

If you haven't before, set minimum goals for prospecting activity:

|  | Month | Week | Day |
|---|---|---|---|
| Prospecting Calls | 575 | 144 | 29 |
| Conversations | 55 | 14 | 3 |
| Appointments | 18 | 5 | 1 |
| Demos | 13 | 3 | 0 |
| Proposals | 7 | 2 | 0 |
| Closed Sales | 4 | 1 | 0 |

## *Month 1*

To optimize your chances of success, I suggest phasing prospecting requirements during a three month period. During the first month, set the productivity goals at 50 percent of the minimum standard.

## *Month 2*

During month two, set the productivity goals at 80 percent of the minimum standard.

## *Month 3*

By month three, hold reps accountable for 100 percent of the new business goal.

> Quick tip: Sales managers may have to adjust the phase-in period based on the average sales cycle of the product or service.

## Compensation plans

The same issue holds true with commissions and/or bonuses. Sales leaders talk about the importance of new business, but stop short of paying for the behavior they want to see through the plan itself.

Let's say company leaders set a minimum new business quota of 15 percent—$75,000 per quarter against a $500,000 goal, and $300,000 annually against a goal of $2,000,000.

Tap into reps' money motivation. With new business being more difficult to close, incent them to pursue it by offering an additional quarterly commission of 1 percent on sales from $75,000 to $150,000 and 2 percent on sales greater than $150,000:

A rep selling $179,000 of new business realizes $1330 in additional commission: $750/$150,000 and $580/$29,000.

Include an annual bonus for those achieving the new business goal. For $300,000, offer a $3,000 bonus, for $300,000–$500,000, offer $5,000 and for $500,000 and above, provide a $7,000 bonus.

Demonstrate commitment to your new business initiative by setting specific goals and rewarding those achieving the targets.

(Note: All numbers shown are examples only. Adjust for your particular business.)

## Policy and procedure

Assessing for skill level, establishing minimum standards, and rewriting the compensation plan help to underscore and support a company's seriousness about new business. Continue the work by drafting specific wording for the sales department policy and procedures manual to address this issue. An example of what you might say includes:

*Sales reps failing to achieve the minimum new business quota for two consecutive quarters will be placed on probation. Any rep failing to achieve the new business quota for a third consecutive quarter must meet with their manager to determine the next course of action—up to and including termination.*

Incorporate verbiage for reps falling below the group average:

*Sales reps falling below the group new business average for two consecutive quarters will be placed on probation. Any rep failing to achieve the group new business average for a third consecutive quarter must meet with their manager to determine the next course of action—up to and including termination.*

Companies with shorter sales cycles may want to add:

*Sales representatives falling below the minimum new business quota or new business group average for two consecutive months twice in the same business year will be subject to termination.*

## Present the plan to executives

Present your plan to your direct supervisor. Likely aware of the new business problem, they will show interest in what you have to say. Consider their thoughts and opinions, and discuss any changes they suggest.

Many sales leaders meet with resistance from their boss when requesting sales assessments and/or sales training. Take the time to explain the importance of each. Enlist their full support.

> Quick tip: Reps held accountable to a new business quota could fail to achieve that goal. Ultimately, this might result in their dismissal. Make certain you and your direct supervisor commit to and see this initiative through—no matter the outcome.

## Address the issue with the rep

When speaking with the rep in question, start with the positive. For example, "Quarter after quarter, you increase business within your existing accounts, like Byt2, by 10 percent or more. Everyone at the company really values your contribution."

Then start a dialogue on where they need to improve. "On the other hand, we've often discussed prospecting and closing new business in your territory. Yet, no new clients come in. What are your thoughts on this?"

Be patient. Let them talk. If they say nothing initially, just let the silence fall. Likely, they'll respond with the usual: "You're right. Last week I dropped in on several companies. The notes are in CRM. I really need to bring in new business."

Be ready. Change occurs here. The two of you engage in a well-honed pattern. You bring up the subject of new business; she wholeheartedly agrees to step up and start delivering. She references CRM notes. You encourage follow-up with these accounts. Nothing happens. The subject gets dropped—for months.

Here's the painful part: She controls this. She's trained you. Her positive and agreeable responses hold you off for up to a full business quarter. She knows what she's doing.

## Switch it up

Break this pattern by:

- Revisiting past promises.
- Comparing her performance to the group's.
- Setting new business goals.

## Past promises

Begin this part of the talk by saying, "I appreciate your efforts to meet new clients. Let's talk about a few of them."

| Date | Time | Account | Notes |
|---|---|---|---|
| 8/29/20xx | 9:04am | Beaumont & Sons | Left message w/ principal David Beaumont's admin |
| 10/03/20xx | 8:35am | White Water Wealth Management | Left voicemail w/ president Cyril Hynes |
| 6/05/20xx | 10:51am | Edusoft | Spoke w/ VP of Product Development. Call back 6 mos. |
| 5/12/20xx | 8:12am | Jackson Landscaping | Sent into email to pres Frank Jackson |
| 2/01/20xx | 9:23am | Green Frog Software | Left voicemail w/ pres Evelyn Li's asst. |
| 12/17/20xx | 10:47am | The Printing Place | Sent intro email to pres Maria Sheller |

Display half a dozen accounts or more. Emphasize the time span of this problem and include accounts from the beginning of her employment through recent days.

"During your early days with us, you contacted Beaumont & Sons. After that initial effort, I don't see another visit in the notes section. About a year and a half ago, you called Edusoft. Again, I see no other follow-up activity. What happens after an initial visit to these accounts?"

Let her talk. Resist filling in silent gaps. Don't wait or hope for a response like, "I really hate cold calling. I find it [scary, intimidating, and/or boring]. I just like working with existing accounts." That won't happen. She knows the stakes here.

Listen to what she has to say. Offer no rebuttal. Move on to the next topic.

## Group performance

Begin with numbers only. Review the tables summarizing new business revenue brought in by their peers. Don't ask for a response.

Continue with a more impactful visual. Let it sink in.

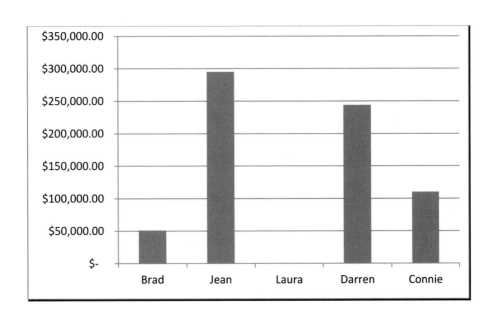

The other reps run the gamut in terms of their performance. It will not be lost on her that every single team member but her brings in *some* new revenue.

## Assessment results

If you choose to assess this rep (or the entire staff), then review the results. Should it show she has solid capabilities in this area, discuss her reluctance to prospect. If the assessment points out weaknesses, address improving her overall skills in any areas mentioned.

Sometimes assessments indicate that a particular rep lacks the innate abilities to prospect. They possess strong skills in other areas, but not in this one. Any training or coaching will result in minimal improvement at best.

Should this prove to be the case, say something along the lines of, "Your struggles with initiating contact with decision-makers and addressing objections makes prospecting difficult. You'd have to work very hard to overcome these limitations. Are you willing to do that?"

## Follow-up meeting

Begin the discussion by saying, "You've had a few days to look at the numbers. What did you think?" Pose an additional questions, like "Did anything come as a surprise?"

Ask frankly, "What stops you from cold calling?" Listen patiently. Give her a few tries to get her thoughts together, but keep repeating the question until you get at least the beginnings of a credible answer.

You've spent several years listening to excuses. Now it's time to be blunt. Have the rep leave this follow-up meeting understanding:

- Her new business revenue falls well short of expectations.
- The situation needs to change.
- She has to be part of that change.

> Quick tip: For valued employees, you could handle this problem through having one rep bring in new business and another serve as account manager.

# Put the issue in writing

Ask the rep to put together a memo outlining their understanding of the discussions thus far. Have them include their plans for addressing this issue.

---

To:        President
From:      Sales Rep
Date:      June 5, 20xx
Re:        New Business

--------------------------------------------------------------------------

During our discussions, I learned the importance of focusing on new business in my territory. I agree to do the following to improve the situation:

- Monitor Jean's and Darren's prospecting calls weekly
- E-mail Ellen a review of my observations
- Set aside the first two hours of every morning for cold calling
- Record all activity in the CRM system
- Place follow-up calls within three days of initial contact
- Conduct two in-person meetings per week with potential new clients
- Ask all current clients for a minimum of two referrals
- Select and discuss a book on cold calling with the director of sales
- Achieve 100 percent of new business quota in three months' time

_____          _____
Salesperson                    Director of Sales
Company X                      Company X

## Ease in

Angry at themselves for tolerating the situation, many sales leaders hand the rep in question a new business quota, then wait to see what happens. Instead, demonstrate your confidence in her by gradually increasing the new revenue goals with time.

You've set the current new business quota at $75,000 per quarter. Consider phasing this in by setting a goal of only $45,000 for the first quarter.

To increase the chances for success during this phase-in period, offer a flat 1 percent on any new business they bring in. Reps appreciate gestures like these and it gives them more motivation to bring in new business.

## Current staff

When speaking to the group, refrain from mentioning individual performance or talent levels. Illustrate *company-wide* new business acquisitions to date through charts and graphs. Emphasize the relevance of new business to company growth and remaining competitive.

Announce recent changes:

- Separate new business quotas
- New compensation plan

To get the sales staff pumped up:

- Create a new business sales contest.
- Give everyone a book on prospecting.

Encourage questions. Listen. Wait to discuss any individual results during one-on-one meetings.

## Top performers

When meeting with these reps in particular, discuss their individual work habits when it comes to new business. Ask questions like:

- What time of day do you typically prospect?
- How much time do you spend prospecting?
- How many calls do you make in that time period?
- Do you use a script(s)?

- What are the most common objections?
- How do you move the process forward?

Keep notes for future coaching sessions, new hire orientation, and staff development.

# Hiring

Managing a sales force able to uncover and close new business involves *hiring* salespeople able to uncover and close new business.

Review your current interview process. Do you inquire about new business acquisition? Ask questions such as:

- What is your cold calling process?
- Do you have a new business quota?
- How many of your current accounts came through your prospecting efforts?
- In your territory, what is the ratio of new to current accounts?

Ask candidates to provide documentation to support their claim. When asking for references, speak to at least one customer they acquired strictly through cold calling.

Throughout the interview process, you'll share information about the:

- Sales revenue quotas (new and existing).
- Structure of the compensation plan (new and existing).

With this, future new hires join your company understanding their prospecting and new business responsibilities.

## New hire orientation

Place a strong emphasis on new business development during the new hires' orientation period. Have them:

- Monitor other reps' prospecting calls.
- Accompany reps to meetings with new prospects.
- Develop a cold calling script.
- Participate in role playing exercises dealing with common objections.

Be cognizant of and manage the new hire's new business activity from the start:

- Get them on the phone prospecting as quickly as possible.
- Read their CRM notes carefully to monitor follow-up activity.
- Meet frequently to discuss any problems.

Focus on new business acquisition early in their tenure. In conversations, acknowledge all successes—big and small.

## Leadership opportunities

Increased business within an existing account isn't new business. Any account not buying from your organization buys from another company.

Effective sales leaders distinguish between, and never confuse, new and existing business. High-performing sales executives hire, train, and manage a staff able to prospect for and close new business. The future of the company you work for, as well as your own job security and promotability, depend on it.

## Summary checklist
## No new business review and checklist

- Clarify problem.
- Research new business productivity staff-wide.
- Retool:
  - Minimum productivity requirements.
  - Compensation plan.
  - Sales policies.
  - Disciplinary action.
  - Interview process.
  - New hire orientation.
- Involve direct supervisor and other executives.
- Speak with nonperforming rep(s).
- Announce changes to current staff.
- Provide appropriate coaching and training.
- Monitor progress.

# Resolution

After their initial discussions about new business, Ellen saw no change whatsoever in Laura's selling habits. She continued on as if nothing had been said. After a week, she finally started making cold calls.

Per their agreement, she worked with Jean and Darren. She sent Ellen an e-mail outlining the discussion. She logged her notes into CRM regularly.

On Wednesday morning of week four, she handed in her resignation. Laura told Ellen Byt2 offered her a position as a senior account manager, working with a business development rep who was responsible for opening new accounts. The senior account manager's responsibilities included increasing business within established accounts.

Ellen had to admit the position sounded perfect for her. She thanked Laura for her contributions with several named accounts. Though sad to lose her, Ellen knew this was for the best. Laura parted from the company professionally and amicably.

Dealing with Laura's lack of prospecting forced Ellen to consider the importance of new business across the entire company. During the weekly staff meeting, the reps take turns leading a discussion on one chapter of the cold calling book she provided. Researching online training comes next. Ellen feels like she and the reps are moving in a positive direction.

# Chapter 3
# Social Media Paralysis

Sales manager Kim watches salesperson Deanna read a profile on LinkedIn, switch to Facebook, then open up another app—one Kim doesn't recognize. This goes on all day, every day.

Kim reviewed current account and new business revenue goals with Deanna during the interview process. Though the company has a strong lead generation program, she told Deanna she couldn't depend on it entirely. She would have to engage in prospecting activity to meet her new business goal of 30 percent of quota.

Describing herself as a social media wizard, Deanna assured Kim that new business acquisition wouldn't be a problem. She described her talent for connecting with hard to reach decision-makers, and proudly presented templates for her response-producing text messages and e-mails.

But her approach to prospecting turned out to involve hours on the Internet researching potential connections to decision-makers, exhaustively researching the potential clients, and spending considerable time creating custom e-mails. A colleague of Kim's calls salespeople like Deanna "librarian reps."

Kim rarely hears Deanna speaking directly to a potential new customer. Current clients were contacted via e-mail. Recently, a longtime customer complained to Kim about never being able to reach Deanna by phone.

Coaching sessions proved disastrous. Deanna dismissed any recommendations, making comments like "No one checks voice mail or picks up the phone anymore. People communicate through text, Web-based apps, and e-mail. That's it."

Despite this, Kim sees potential. Deanna knows the value of introductions and understanding a prospect's unique needs. Unlike a lot of reps, new and tenured, she knows her job involves closing deals and exceeding revenue targets.

Too much gets spent time researching companies. And Deanna overestimated actual e-mail response rates, and underestimated the high volume of reps trying to leverage connections to meet decision-makers. The value of mixing things up and using the auto-dialer to call customers and prospects eluded her completely.

Deanna's social media approach to sales wouldn't be a problem at all— if it was successful. But it isn't. She's behind on both her new and renewal business quotas. As Deanna stares at her computer screen, looking almost mesmerized, Kim wonders how to begin.

---

### Problem summary

Sales representative

- Works diligently
- Spends too much time on the Internet
- Depends on social media to meet prospects
- Exhibits weak phone sales skills
- Misses quota for new and renewal business

---

Sales manager
- Thinks the rep has potential
- Coaches and makes suggestions, but meets with resistance
- Wants to see her:
  - Balance use of Internet and social media with other approaches
  - Develop better phone sales skills
  - Initiate live conversations with prospects

---

This sales leader not only supervises a rep spending an inordinate amount of time doing research, but one holding strong opinions and biases as well. Reps with this personality tend to resist coaching and direction from supervisors. They consider making changes only when:

- Presented with objective data.
- Shown a different way to do things by their peers.

Keep this in mind as you put your plan together.

# Getting started

As a beginning point, look at sales versus goal for the entire sales staff. How does this rep's performance compare?

| | Quota | Actual | Difference | Percentage Difference |
|---|---|---|---|---|
| **Marissa** | $ 1,300,000 | $ 1,489,000 | $ 189,000 | 15% |
| **Cathryn** | $ 1,250,000 | $ 1,346,000 | $ 96,000 | 8% |
| **Ramon** | $ 1,390,000 | $ 1,665,000 | $ 275,000 | 20% |
| **Deanna** | $ 1,100,000 | $ 879,000 | $ (221,000) | -20% |
| **Nick** | $ 1,295,000 | $ 1,200,400 | $ (94,600) | -7% |
| **William** | $ 1,320,000 | $ 1,532,000 | $ 212,000 | 16% |
| **Totals** | $ 7,655,000 | $ 8,111,400 | $ 456,400 | 6% |

Next, focus on new business. How does the group perform against their new business quota?

| | Quota | New Business Goal (30%) | Actual | Percentage Difference |
|---|---|---|---|---|
| **Marissa** | $ 1,300,000 | $ 390,000 | $ 422,000 | 8% |
| **Cathryn** | $ 1,250,000 | $ 375,000 | $ 394,000 | 5% |
| **Ramon** | $ 1,390,000 | $ 417,000 | $ 510,000 | 22% |
| **Deanna** | $ 1,100,000 | $ 330,000 | $ 146,000 | -56% |
| **Nick** | $ 1,295,000 | $ 388,500 | $ 354,000 | -9% |
| **William** | $ 1,320,000 | $ 396,000 | $ 408,000 | 3% |
| **Totals** | **$ 7,655,000** | $ 2,296,500 | **$ 2,234,000** | -3% |

Though not the only rep to miss their new business goal (Nick missed his goal as well), Deanna comes in 56 percent under quota. Had she achieved her new business target of $330,000, the group moves from –3 percent to exceeding the new business quota by 5 percent.

Ramon leads the group in exceeding both his overall and new business revenue goals. Either run a CRM report or talk to him about any recently closed new business deals and find out how he initially came across the prospect. Was it through a referral, lead, or cold call? How did he first make contact: e-mail, voice mail, phone call, or social media?

| Customer | Source |
|---|---|
| Catalina Equipment | Lead |
| Ace Delivery Service | Prospect call |
| Marcon Construction | Customer referral |
| iSource | Lead |
| Young & Davidson Corp | Lead |
| Analytic Docs | Prospect call |

More than 30 percent of Ramon's new business comes directly from prospecting calls. Ask other reps on staff about their approach to new business. Do they have a system? If so, what is it? Find out how social media factors in.

## Tracking activity

Virtually every employee uses the Internet, social media, and search engines on some level. Consider using a time-tracking app to gain greater insight into what percentage of the day reps spend connected and how they use that time.

Look at the Internet connection times and auto-dial times for the higher- and lower-performing reps. See if a correlation exists. The better reps might spend more or less time connected to the Internet or the phone than the ones who struggle. The reverse could be true.

Use this information to better understand time management, spot problem areas, develop insights, and adapt best practices for technology usage.

## Create a plan

Revisit minimum productivity standards for the sales department. Update the list to recognize all forms of modern and traditional prospecting (e-mails, Skype, texts, LinkedIn, phone calls, online demos).

If you've gotten out of the habit of monitoring the reps' productivity versus the goals, make more of an effort going forward.

## Training

Younger salespeople might not have spent a great deal of time speaking on the phone, preferring to text and e-mail instead. Unfortunately for some, this can translate to poor phone skills.

Knowing this, don't waste time watching the reps struggle with the phone conversations. Whether field or phone-based or a combination of the two, salespeople need solid skills in this area. Research inside sales training courses focused on telephone skills (online or classroom-based), and select the one that works best for your organization. Enroll struggling reps in the course.

## Present the plan to executives

When meeting with your direct supervisor, avoid focusing the discussion on one salesperson in particular. Instead, broaden the conversation. Discuss technology in the workplace and trends you've observed as they relate to sales, such as:

- Increasing dependence on social media.
- Over reliance on e-mail.
- Reluctance to pick up the phone.
- Poor time management.

Review the charts you've put together. Talk about what you discovered in terms of how the reps find and make contact with prospects. Discuss how some reps hesitate to pick up the phone. Make the recommendation that any rep struggling with this skill get enrolled in an inside sales training course as soon as they start with your organization. Share the list of providers, discussing the pros and cons of each.

Understandably, supervisors might question the ROI for these courses. If so, I recommend emphasizing reduced ramp-up time. Mention the number of hours reps currently spend on the Internet and writing e-mails.

Make the argument that stronger phone skills would increase both their confidence and the likelihood of their calling prospects. This could help shorten the time between the first day on the job and the closing of that first sale. If you don't have any data to back this up, offer to track it with the next few new hires.

## Address the issue with the rep

Managers in this situation often think to themselves, "If I could get them off the Internet and on the phone, we'd solve this problem." If only it were that simple. Really, you're dealing with four separate issues with this salesperson:

- Failing to achieve sales revenue goals
- Struggling with time management
- Feeling uncomfortable using the phone as a sales tool
- Holding strong opinions about modern-day selling

Especially with opinionated reps who resist coaching, several conversations may transpire before they open up to what you have to say. At the same time, you need them to produce, so don't let a long time elapse between each conversation. Move the whole process along.

## Initial conversation

For this first meeting, I recommend not comparing reps' sales numbers to those of the other salespeople. Leave that for another time. With their strongly held convictions, they might get defensive.

Just get their thoughts on pre-call research. Ask questions like:

- How much and what type of information do they need before calling an existing customer?
- What about a prospect?
- How much time do they think it should take to get that information?
- Overall, what percentage of their day should be spent doing online research?
- What percentage should be spent speaking to customers?

Some reps struggle with differentiating between research done prior to certain conversations or activities such as:

- An introductory call.
- An existing customer call.
- A meeting or presentation.

Get their opinion on the amount of time needed for each.

After the conversation, give them some time to consider what you've spoken about. Don't give them an assignment, but schedule a follow-up meeting for a few days later.

## Second conversation

Begin by asking the rep if she has given any thought to the discussion of a few days ago. See what she has to say. Let her know you honor her opinions on social media and pre-call research, e-mails, and phone communications.

Present the tables comparing her sales performance to the other reps. Get her thoughts.

Though she hasn't produced the desired results, Deanna works hard. Undoubtedly, she admires Ramon's success. Leveraging her respect for what her peers have to say, use a visual to show what percentage of Ramon's new business originates from leads, referrals, and cold calls.

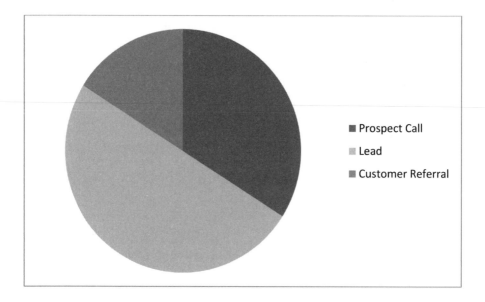

This objective information from a peer will make an impression.

Capitalize on the rep's respect for objective data by showing them a chart or graph from an independent source, such as the one on the next page.

Move the meeting toward the end goal by saying something like, "We've talked about the importance of hitting quota. Although you're putting in a lot of effort and using some creative approaches to meet prospects, you're struggling to achieve your revenue goals."

Ask her to come up with two actionable ideas for improving the situation. Though difficult, resist the urge to assign these action items yourself or appear disappointed in the ones they choose. Have a little patience and let the process unfold. Agree to review the results during the next meeting. Schedule it right then and there.

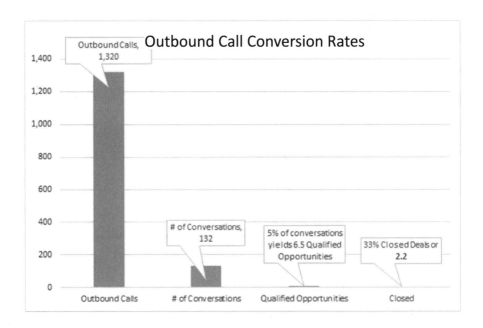

Call conversion statistics provided by the American Association of Inside Sales Professionals (AA-ISP).

Quick tip: At some point during difficult conversations like these, take a moment to talk about why you hired a rep to begin with. Enumerate what you see as their strengths. Add to this by mentioning positive comments made by other reps and department leaders. This helps a lot with instilling confidence.

## Third conversation

Find out how they thought they did with respect to the two action items. Gauge their energy. Do they seem excited, ambivalent, or disappointed in the results? As with round one, encourage them to talk as much as possible. You should start to get a sense of their attitude.

## Positive signs

If they're beginning to see they need a more multifaceted approach to customer communication, they might be open to making some changes.

Don't step in and coach them just yet. Instead, schedule time for them to work alongside those reps who use good judgment on account research, regularly achieve their revenue goals, and have good phone skills.

Tell the observing rep you expect them to come away from these sessions with an understanding of their peers' approach to:

- Introducing themselves to prospects.
- Integrating technology into their sales process.
- Managing their time.
- Conducting pre-call research.

Meet with the rep being observed beforehand and talk to them about what you'd like to see accomplished in these sessions.

## Reluctant rep

When they don't appear to be getting on the bus at all, be straightforward. Tell them you're questioning whether or not they have the ability to meet their sales revenue goals. Ask outright about their willingness to work with you to correct this problem. Let them know they need to show immediate improvement in:

- Reducing time on the Internet.
- Defining adequate customer research.
- Communicating with customers through a variety of methods.
- Picking up the phone regularly.
- Demonstrating improved time management.

If they insist their approach will lead to success, remind them it hasn't happened yet.

> Quick tip: If a rep continues to resist coaching, make reading a book on inside sales mandatory. Continue to try to work with them one-on-one, but do not sign them up for training. Every year, companies waste money training reps that aren't

bought in nor have little interest. Save your budget and the instructor's time. It simply won't work—at least not now.

# Coaching

When working directly with reps, I talk to them about making a distinction between initial research (prior to a prospecting call) and in-depth research (necessary before a presentation). Prior to contacting a prospect, I recommend they spend 10 minutes or so learning about the company. My suggestions include looking at the Website, and reading one or two recent press releases and maybe a few blog posts.

In the notes column of the CRM, I propose writing a brief description about what the company does. Include links to information that proved valuable. If reps can't reach the decision-maker and want to try to contact them again at some later point, they won't have to conduct the research all over again.

# Final conversation

Whether reps in this situation begin to embrace the manager's advice or not, ask them to create a plan for solving this problem. Both of you should sign and date it.

---

To:        Sales Manager
From:      Sales Rep
Date:      October 19, 20xx
Re:        New Business

------------------------------------------------------------------------

After talking with my manager about spending less time doing online research and more time speaking to customers directly, I will:

- Listen to one rep's customer calls each week for one hour
- Spend 10–15 minutes researching a company before calling

- Log research information into CRM
- Use the introduction/voice-mail message we created
- Read and discuss one chapter of the inside sales book each week
- Create and stick to a daily schedule for calling
- Increase calling time by 10 minutes each day
- Meet weekly with manager to discuss progress

———————————————    ———————————————
Salesperson                    Sales Manager
Company X                      Company X

Let them know that if they aren't at or above quota or at or above the group average by (select an appropriate date), you will have no choice but to put them on warning. (See "Create a Plan" in Chapter 1: The Inconsistent Sales Rep for additional information.)

## Current staff

In preparation for informed discussions with the rep in question, you've done a lot of research. After reading some of the reports, you now know whether this issue affects the entire group or only one or two salespeople.

If most of the reps hit their revenue goals and use technology judiciously, and customers aren't complaining about a lack of personal contact, the problem isn't widespread. Deal with the one or two who seem to be struggling with this issue.

When a staff-wide problem exists, first meet with each rep individually. Discuss their performances and problems around time management, customer contact, and technology. Use the same approach to improving the situation as you did with the first rep.

## Staff meetings

Everything evolves and changes with time, sales being no exception. Highly effective managers provide a continuous learning environment, revisiting and improving upon the basics of sales, while embracing new ideas and technology.

Use staff meetings as an educational platform. Ask reps with strong phone skills to share their techniques. Set up role-playing exercises for the group. Have those doing a good job of time management discuss their approach. All reps probably have a strength or two to contribute to the group.

Open up a discussion of technology. Ask the reps which programs, software, and apps:

- Provide the most benefit?
- Feel like a waste of time?
- Could they not live without?
- Would they like to see the company invest in?

Begin to understand their thoughts about the role they see technology playing and how you can best equip them for 21st-century sales.

# Hiring

In the interview process, ask questions that paint the clearest picture possible of how applicants organize their sales day.

## Scheduling

- Can you break your day down for me in terms of time spent speaking with customers, researching companies, and entering information into CRM?
- By what time of day are you usually on the phone or in front of a customer?

## Interacting with customers

- When was the last time you picked up the phone or dropped into an office spontaneously and tried to make contact with a decision-maker?
- How do you utilize voice mail and the telephone or Skype?

## Research

- When you prepare to call a customer for the first time, what is your pre-call preparation like? What do you feel you need to know to make that initial call?

- Tell me about the most valuable technology tool you use for sales purposes.
- Of all the tools available to you, which do you think adds the least value?

Describe to the rep how you see their sales day as they explained it to you. Then ask a recap question like, "Have I got that at least mostly right?" Let them add anything they see fit. Conclude the interview process feeling as if you can visualize them during an average sales day.

## New hire orientation

When scheduling new hires' time for the first few weeks, allocate as many hours as possible for them to work with and observe high-performing reps. Make sure these reps discuss their use of different tools to succeed at their job.

In terms of organizing your own day, leave space in the calendar to work with new hires frequently. Provide tips and coaching on Internet research and social media in sales. Get a sense of their mastery of sales fundamentals beyond the technology space.

## Leadership opportunities

A lot of sales executives manage reps ranging in age from their 20s through their 60s. These reps came of age professionally in different eras, using different devices and methodologies to achieve their sales quotas.

Most supervise both reps in their 20s who spend all their time connected to Wi-Fi and older reps possibly struggling with certain aspects of technology. The younger group might wrestle with more traditional sales skills, whereas the older group retains strong relationships with long-term clients.

Each generation has a great deal to offer. Sales executives able to provide direction, interact with, motivate, and coach these different generations possess a valuable modern day set of skills.

## Summary checklist
### Social media paralysis review and checklist

- Clarify problem.
- Observe the rep's work habits.
- Gather the facts about:

- Performance vs. quota.
- Time spent on social media.
- Present plan to direct supervisor.
- Understand the rep's approach to the job.
- Appreciate different generational views on technology.
- Provide coaching and guidance.

## Resolution

Kim watched as Deanna, the featured presenter at the weekly staff meeting, addressed her fellow sales reps about the use of social media in the sales process.

The other salespeople showed interest and asked a lot of questions. When she was finished, they applauded with gusto. Kim could see Deanna was proud. Several months ago, she guessed neither one of them would have predicted this positive outcome.

When Kim first started talking to Deanna about her disappointing sales performance, they ended up in an uncomfortable stand-off. Deanna felt certain she would succeed with her social media-dominated sales approach. Kim disagreed.

At Kim's insistence, Deanna began observing and working with the other sales reps, seeing how they approached customers in their territories. At the same time, she asked her to read a book on inside sales, which they discussed together during one-on-one meetings.

Gradually, Deanna began to see the one-sidedness of her sales plan. During an observation session, a rep referred to her as a tech-snob. Although he said it jokingly, she knew he meant it. Another asked if her reluctance to pick up the phone involved a fear of rejection. Deanna gave that some serious thought.

Slowly, she started to accept coaching from Kim. Together, they created an introduction and voice-mail message she felt comfortable with. The phone began to seem like less and less of a threat and more like another tool to accomplish her goals.

One day, after calling on a customer, she considered the advice of one of her colleagues. "After speaking with a customer," he said, "ask them if they know of anyone else in their network who might be interested in speaking with you about our product."

Though Deanna's heart pounded as she asked the customer that question, to her surprise they neither hung up nor seemed annoyed. The customer told her he couldn't think of anyone right off, but to ask him next time they spoke.

Deanna typed his response verbatim into her notes section. She would ask him that same question next time, a thought she found both scary and exhilarating.

# Chapter 4
# Salesperson Fiefdom

Two years after she started her bioscience firm, CEO and PhD Theresa hired Ben as the first sales rep. Since that time he has been the company's one and only salesperson. He calls on all current customers, and receives and follows up on any incoming leads.

Ben's former employer, a big player in the same industry, laid him off after being acquired by another company. With the experience and contacts they desperately needed, Theresa decided to call him. Her hands shook as she dialed his cell phone number, worried that a rep of his caliber would find the idea of working for her small company ridiculous.

To her great surprise, he agreed to speak with her about the opportunity. After several discussions, she made him an offer. Though he asked for a generous compensation package, she felt he was worth it—and he proved to be.

Ben exceeds all his quotas. In the three years he's been with the company, Theresa has never dealt with a customer complaint. When he's in the office, he's friendly to everyone. Theresa has learned a lot from him about sales and the business world.

To grow her company, Theresa must hire additional salespeople. She's both excited and fearful about taking her business to another level. Any concerns she has pale in comparison to her trepidation of dealing with Ben.

The first time she approached him about expanding the sales team, he convinced her not to. He said there was really only enough business for one and a quarter reps. He promised to increase revenue by 30 percent in the largest accounts. She let the matter drop. With his business acumen, she assumed he must know.

A year later, pressured by her investors, she talked to him about it again. He told her, in a rather abrupt tone, that if she hired another rep and gave them any of his accounts, he would walk out the door. "Recruiters call me all the time," he said. "It won't be a problem."

Theresa knows Ben cannot handle any additional accounts. But what if she divides up the accounts, hires another rep, Ben leaves, and that rep turns out to be a disaster? Then what? She's heard horror stories from her executive team about trying to find good reps. She feels trapped.

---

### **Problem summary**

Sales rep
- Exceeds sales goals
- Is well respected by customers
- Resists losing territory/accounts
- Uses manipulative and threatening tactics

Manager
- Pleased with rep's performance
- Pressured to expand the sales force
- Reluctant to upset the rep by adjusting sales territories

At a certain point, growth-oriented companies need sales forces of a certain size to reach their sales goals and must add salespeople. No one salesperson, no matter how talented and experienced, helps a company achieve next level growth single-handedly.

On the way to achieving these aggressive targets, some companies get held hostage by one rep. This means negotiating and compromising their way out of this tricky situation, taking their power back in stages.

## Getting started

Without realizing it, company leaders sometimes act as if they're asking the reps for *permission* to expand the sales force, and then back off when they object. Now, you'll be *telling* them what's going to happen. To succeed, be prepared.

Begin this project by gathering accurate market information. Ask investors, colleagues, and professional associations for advice about the best sources. Where necessary, spend money for valid, relevant data. Gain a solid understanding of the:

- Size of the market for your product/service.
- Number of companies purchasing these goods.
- Current and potential market share for your size company.

With this information, forecast company growth for the next five years.

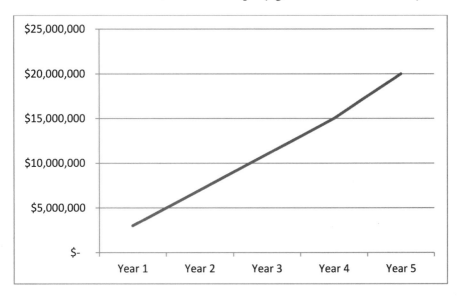

Next, list the companies with which you want to start doing business. Estimate five-year revenue predictions for each.

Ask questions such as:

- Which of our competitors do they buy from currently?
- Do we have any contacts there?
- Where are they located?
- Which territory should they be assigned to?
- How many reps will be needed to call on these accounts?

## Peers

When concerned about a serious problem, business and sales leaders often forget the most obvious source of advice: their peers. Ask friends, associates, and colleagues if they know someone who faced a similar situation. With this being a common problem, you'll probably have two or three people to call before you know it.

Find out how they increased the size of their sale force. How did discussions with the rep go? What mistakes did they make? What would they do over again if they could? What went well, or at least better than expected? Listen to their experiences and use it to inform and guide your decisions in this process.

## Hiring a replacement

Speak with recruiters placing reps in your particular field. Have a conversation with a few candidates. If you want to run an ad instead and interview candidates yourself, think about the time involved. Do you have the staff to handle it in-house or should you outsource some of the work to a contract recruiter?

Sales reps sometimes make good on their promise to resign—especially the best ones. Educate yourself about viable replacements should this occur. This rep has threatened to quit if you add to the sales staff. Hope that he doesn't, but plan for it to happen.

## Titles

When you hire one or more additional salespeople, fiefdom reps expect their tenure and contribution to the company to be recognized. For many, this means asking for an upgraded title. Especially when they have made major contributions like significantly increasing revenue or closing a major account, you can see their side of things.

Typically, managers get caught off guard by the request, hastily agreeing to an inappropriate title. Think about what makes sense before having any conversations with the rep.

Unless you plan to give them supervisory responsibility over any new hires, do not agree to titles like: sales manager, director of sales, or vice president of sales. If they express interest in a management position, tell them you will take that under consideration once the sales staff reaches a certain size, but not at this time.

Designations like senior sales representative or major account sales representative, among others, make solid choices. Upgrading a rep's title acknowledges their contributions and gives them elevated, but appropriate, status.

> Quick tip: If they already have a VP title, look at the recommendations for this situation in Chapter 14: Unqualified Vice President of Sales.

## Financial incentives

In a case where you really want salespeople to stay, offer an attractive compensation upgrade. Consider the potential costs of replacing versus retaining them. Together with a business partner or a board of directors, look into additional stock options or bonuses. Work with a lawyer or CPA to draw up and formalize the offer.

## Meet customers

Business leaders put in long hours running the company. If they hear no complaints from customers, sometimes they choose to leave well enough alone, making little effort to visit or get to know them.

The panic a lot of leaders feel when dealing with the fiefdom rep stems from having no independent relationship with clients. Of course they worry about the rep quitting and taking the business with them to their next employer. It's a valid concern. Little ties the client to the company beyond their connection with the rep.

Prior to speaking with the rep about expanding the sales force, get out and interact with customers. Make some visits on your own, meeting with whomever your rep calls on and other C-level executives when possible. Ask the rep to schedule other visits for the two of you. Observe how they handle themselves when in front of the customer.

Fiefdom reps like to maintain control, telling managers things like, "That buyer has told me on several occasions that she's too busy for the dog and pony show sales call from executives."

Stand your ground. Remind the rep these are the company's clients, not theirs. Most customers appreciate executives taking time out to meet with them. It allows them to speak their mind about products or services and learn a few things about your company.

# Training

Frequently overlooked or forgotten, training and development provides a valuable negotiation tool. Reps working solo lack peers to bounce ideas off of and learn from. Although you meet with them one-on-one, you don't hold formal sales meetings.

No matter how hard-working or talented, all reps need to revisit the basics and get exposure to new ideas. Look into available programs or courses. Be sure to select those that match their experience level. Most appreciate the gesture very much.

## Present the plan to executives

Tackling this problem involves dealing with several issues at the same time:

- Reorganizing the sales department.
- Hiring additional reps.
- Negotiating with a current employee.

When meeting with an adviser, a boss, investors, or a board of directors, organize your recommendations into separate phases.

Reinforce your overall satisfaction with the salesperson and the desire to retain him. It might help to review some of the rep's major accomplishments. At the same time, speak candidly about his possible departure.

> Quick tip: This problem has applications for sales executives as well. Imagine a VP of North American sales having to split territories and grow from five reps to six. She would face many of the same issues.

# Phase I

Based on the market information you've gathered, discuss and finalize:

- The number of reps to hire.
- During what period of time.
- Territory/customer realignments.

To increase the chances of the current rep remaining with the company, agree on:

- Details of the new hire compensation plan.
- Two or three training vendors.
- Several choices for an upgraded title.

Work out the details, but leave room for negotiation. The rep might not necessarily accept the first offer.

# Phase II

With a specific strategy in place, talk more seriously about the potential of the rep resigning. Mention your concerns about the lack of a personal relationship with many of the clients. Recommend that before speaking to the rep you:

- Visit clients alone and with the sales rep.
- Talk to a recruiter about sales candidates.

# Phase III

Finally, brainstorm for ideas about the best way to open up discussions with the salesperson. Many investors or those on a board have dealt with this situation before. Listen to their thoughts and suggestions prior to approaching the salesperson.

## Address the issue with the rep

Get right to it. Say to the rep, "Ben, during the next five years, we would like to grow the company to $20 million. To accomplish that goal, I've made the decision to expand the size of our sales force, starting by hiring four reps during those five years. I'd like to share some information with you."

If they start to object, interrupt. Strike first by bringing up his threatening to quit. It diminishes his power over you and the organization. This lets him know you've thought it over, understand the possibility of it happening, and want to move ahead anyway.

Try a statement along the lines of, "I know you've mentioned quitting or going to the competition if we hire additional reps. We would hate to lose you. But you can't single-handedly call on and grow all of the accounts we want to do business with. No one person could. We're expanding the sales force and hope you'll want to be a part of our growth. Are you interested in hearing me out?"

This last phrase will catch their attention. Use it verbatim.

Some leaders worry about reps quitting right then and there if they take this approach. Though fiefdom salespeople in this situation could resign within a few days or weeks, it's highly unlikely they'll walk right out the door after you make this statement. At the very least, they'll be curious about what you have to say.

If they do threaten to quit at any point during conversation, ask them outright, "Is this a resignation? Are you resigning as of this moment?" That usually calms them right down. But be careful of your tone. Say it sympathetically, not aggressively.

## Private and confidential

As a starting point for most discussions, I advise leaders to provide the reps with facts and figures on company growth projections and account lists, let them review the data, then have a follow-up conversation.

Take appropriate precautions.

In past conversations, this rep has threatened to quit. You certainly don't want them leaving with proprietary information and potentially handing it to a competitor or current customers, using it as leverage.

Be judicious about the information you share. Look at it together on your computer screen or create a presentation. Don't e-mail it to them or provide a copy. If they request a copy, remind them of their threat to resign.

## Discussing changes

Ask that reps listen to the sales plan in its entirety. After that point, assure them you'll hear what they have to say uninterrupted. This benefits you in two ways. One, they learn about the whole package you've put together. They'll realize the organization's commitment to these changes and to their career. Secondly, the hiring of additional reps might not be as dire a situation as they pictured.

First, present the market information. Most reps have decent business acumen. Seeing independent facts and figures might bring them around to seeing things from the organization's point of view.

Next, review the realigned geographic territories, along with the breakdown by account rep. Show any new assignments of major accounts.

Share the five-year revenue forecast. This illustrates the gap between what the company believes they have the potential to generate through that period of time versus the sales revenue realized from five reps in total (themselves included).

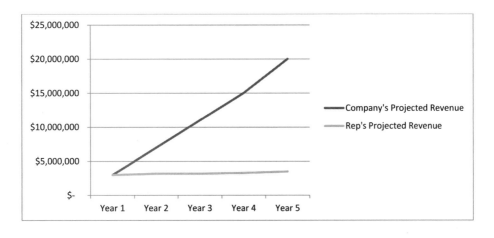

Listen to what they have to say.

Finish with a discussion of the upgraded benefits and compensation plan. Include training and the suggested new title(s) as part of that package.

## Income

Although fiefdom reps have many reasons for wanting to maintain the status quo, worries about their earning potential top the list. Most see losing territory or accounts as losing money.

To assuage their concerns, show them a list of a few accounts you believe have solid growth potential if worked effectively.

| Account | Current Revenue | Five Year Revenue Prediction | Difference |
|---|---|---|---|
| Snider-Mason | $ 20,000 | $ 150,000 | $ 130,000 |
| Calonton | $ 4,000 | $ 39,000 | $ 35,000 |
| Blue Monkey | $ 18,700 | $ 92,500 | $ 73,800 |
| iWelcome | $ 43,000 | $ 100,000 | $ 57,000 |
| Farmington Electric | $ 10,120 | $ 74,500 | $ 64,380 |
| Totals | $ 95,820 | $ 456,000 | $ 360,180 |

## Concluding the conversation

At this point, reps have a lot of thoughts running through their head. Solo reps often do quite a bit of traveling, sometimes calling on larger companies all across the country. Understandably, they might be disappointed about working a smaller territory and giving up some marquee accounts.

Some might share their thoughts about the plans right away, whereas others need some time. If they express interest in thinking things over, agree to it. But let them know you want to get started on hiring reps and you'll need to have an answer from them within two business days.

If they seem like they want to start negotiating right away, that's fine. Refrain from agreeing to anything until you review any requests with your manager, investors, advisers, or board. Let them know you'll get back to them in a reasonable period of time.

Conclude the discussion positively. Assure them the hiring of additional reps has nothing to do with their performance, with which you've been very pleased. Reinforce this being about company growth.

Mention specific accomplishments: "I thought about starting a company like this in grad school. The president of Linear Scientific spoke at my graduation. Among many others, you used your connections and sales skills to open that account. I still can't believe we do business with Linear. I appreciate all you've done for us and look forward to working with you for many years to come. I hope you'll be staying with us."

# Negotiating

Most high-performing reps understand how to negotiate. If solo salespeople ask for more than you offered initially, consider their demands. Agree to what you can. Everyone likes to win a round or two.

When their requests exceed your comfort level, say something like, "We feel letting you keep these six customers jeopardizes the five-year growth plan. Given all the list of customers you'll be calling on, we don't think you'll be able to effectively increase sales revenue within those companies."

Try to deny as few requests as possible. But when you do say no, make it about future company growth.

# Follow-up conversation

Reps might ask for concessions above and beyond what was agreed to by the board or investors, leaving you unable to come to terms. They could tender their resignation outright. In either case, work out their last day of employment.

If you agree to terms, end the discussion on a high note. Reiterate how pleased you are to be able to work this out. Emphasize this by asking about their willingness to:

- Participate in the interview process for new reps.
- Offer suggestions for training and orientation.

Once they've decided to remain with the organization, most reps agree to be part of that process.

# Hiring

Before they meet the solo rep, let candidates know the current sales department consists of only one rep right now. Briefly discuss a few of his accomplishments and his involvement in the training process.

When an applicant might take over one of his accounts, ask:

- Have you ever taken over an account previously called on by another rep from the same company?
- How was the situation handled?

If the current rep agrees to interview the prospective candidates, don't leave it to chance. Discuss the situation with him beforehand. Get an understanding of what he'll be asking. Make suggestions or request rephrasing of certain questions.

# New hire orientation

In any industry or with any sized company, current reps have the best suggestions for structuring orientation. Having been the new employee themselves, and in the case of the fiefdom rep, the only salesperson, seek their counsel.

Find out about their early experiences in the position. What information did they need but didn't get? What did they find to be very helpful? Did they work closely with any other employees? If so, what did they learn? Have they seen changes in the market during their time with the company?

Using their suggestions, put together an orientation schedule for the new hires that helps them acclimate to their new organization as quickly as possible.

# Speak with the current staff

Lone reps get into the habit of doing their own thing. Often direct supervisors, who chat with them on a regular basis, see no need for formal meetings. As new reps join the company, start holding regular sales staff meetings complete with an agenda. If reps work in different cities, have the meeting by Skype or conference call.

Ask your senior rep, along with other knowledgeable employees, to make regular presentations about customers, products, competitors, or the market. Select a book for the reps to read. Discuss one chapter at each meeting, with the reps taking turns leading the conversation. Emphasize continuous learning and sales development.

Well-run, organized sales staff meetings help leaders transition from the one rep company to a cohesive group of salespeople.

## Leadership opportunities

I frequently consult with organizations where one rep runs the show. As challenging as the reps' actions might be at times, the idea of their quitting causes these executives even greater anxiety.

Negotiating with and retaining fiefdom reps requires courage and planning. Taking on this salesperson is not for the risk averse. But doing so provides the company with the opportunity to create a real, functioning sales department and grow the business.

## Summary checklist
### Salesperson fiefdom review and checklist

- Clarify problem.
- Research:
  - Market size
  - Recruitments firms
- Determine hiring needs.
- Visit valued clients.
- Accompany the rep on customer visits.
- Create a plan to incent the rep to stay.
- Discuss the situation and present the offer to the rep.
- Negotiate.
- Hire and onboard a new rep.
- Transition accounts.

# Resolution

Ben acted surprisingly calm when Theresa presented him with the sales force expansion plan. There were no threats of quitting or promises to sell more. Instead, he comported himself like someone who had gotten their way for as long as they could.

After thinking Theresa's offer over, he countered by asking for the title of vice president of sales, a larger base salary, a higher commission rate, and more stock options. He did not express any interest in managing the new reps.

Theresa said no to the vice president title and a higher base salary, but increased his stock options and added an additional tier to the compensation plan. If he exceeded a certain dollar amount each quarter, Ben would earn an extra 2 percent commission. They agreed on senior sales representative as an appropriate title.

Although he appreciated the opportunity, Ben asked if the money allocated for training could instead be put toward his joining a local professional sales organization. This group held bi-weekly breakfast meetings featuring interesting speakers and he felt he would gain more from it overall rather than a one-off training session.

Though she thought he might be using his new contacts in this organization for job-hunting purposes, she agreed to it. She realized if he was going to quit someday, he would do so when he was ready.

Toward the end of their talk, Theresa brought up the possibility of Ben's taking part in the interview and orientation process for the new reps. She told him that with all his experience and market knowledge, he had a lot to offer. Ben agreed. Theresa sensed he might even be looking forward to it.

# Chapter 5
# Trouble With Titles

During his final interview for the open sales position, Aaron requested the title of solutions consultant. Carolyn, the director of sales, was taken aback. Everyone on the sales staff had the title of sales representative.

He told Carolyn "sales representative" elicited an initial negative response, and resistance from potential customers. The title didn't reflect his close work with the company's sales engineers to customize solutions for his clients.

Several decades older than Aaron and wanting to work well with him, Carolyn agreed to the request. As long as he achieved quota, she reasoned, what did it really matter? Maybe the title of sales representative was passé.

After his first few weeks on the job, several clients called, inquiring about their new solutions consultant. What were his job responsibilities?

Would they be working with two people—Aaron and a salesperson? Would the level of service be the same as before?

Brad, her most tenured sales rep and unofficial new hire trainer, stormed into her office demanding that his title be changed to grand chief ambassador. He informed her he no longer wanted to help train Aaron who wasn't making any friends with his "above it all attitude."

Carolyn winced at Brad's statement. She knew it was true. Aaron never missed an opportunity to mention his title—both to customers and his fellow reps. He sometimes acted as if he were in a new division of the company, one created just for him.

Then there was Molly. Several months ago, she approached Carolyn about the possibility of handling only large accounts and being promoted to national account rep. Sophisticated and astute, Molly knew how to navigate the big accounts, and open up new business in different departments.

Carolyn didn't want to lose Molly, but found the title a little too big for an organization their size. To justify the position, she would have to make territory changes. This might be as unpopular with the reps as the solutions consultant debacle. To avoid making a decision, she's been putting Molly off.

How did titles get to be so problematic?

---

### Problem summary

Director of sales

- Must address the whole issue of titles
- Mistakenly agreed to a new title to satisfy the rep
- Stalls on another title request to avoid a second mistake

Customers

- Confused by unfamiliar title of the new rep
- Need clarification of the rep's responsibilities

Sales representatives

- Asking for special titles/designations

> - Requesting titles that are not a good fit for the company
>
> Sales staff
> - Resent unique title given to the new rep

Clients calling a company receive clear direction from the voice prompts: Press one for Sales, press two for Customer Service, press three for Accounts Payable. Websites offer separate and distinct tabs: About, Product, and Contact Us.

Sales leaders need to make it easy for the customer to do business with their organization. If one sales rep's title baffles customers, and another has a title that overstates their responsibilities, little good comes of the situation.

When interviewing salespeople, I often have to dig for information due to nondescript titles like:

- Territory manager.
- Business development specialist.
- Marketing representative.
- Account manager.

My questions include asking if they:

- Have a quota?
- Manage other salespeople?
- Cold call exclusively?
- Cover a geographic territory?

Look at this situation as an opportunity to reconsider the whole idea of titles. Modernize while maintaining accurate, readily understood designations that help those in and outside of a company navigate the organization.

## Getting started

Consider every rep in your group individually. What are their responsibilities? Are they similar or different? How so?

Separate their responsibilities, length of service, and talents:

| Rep | Current Title | Years of Experience | Tenure | Area of Specialty |
|-----|---------------|---------------------|--------|-------------------|
| Brad | Sales Representative | 35 | 21 years | Tenured; Mentoring new reps |
| Molly | Sales Representative | 10 | 2 years | Large accounts |
| Jonah | Sales Representative | 6 | 4 years | No specialty |
| Deirdre | Sales Representative | 15 | 9 years | Tenured; No specialty |
| Aaron | Solutions Consultant | 3 | < 1 year | No specialty |

Managers completing this exercise often realize they haven't contemplated the reps' tenure and unique contributions in a long time—or ever.

Several years ago, Brad talked to Carolyn about feeling bored (common with senior reps). He didn't want to change jobs. He didn't want a different job. He just felt unchallenged.

She started integrating him into new hire orientation. Together, they collaborated on a training manual. Brad worked with all new reps first. He felt more energized and served as a fantastic mentor to the new reps.

Because the company had only five reps and Brad's primary responsibility was selling, she never considered a title change.

Molly, though only with the company a few years, has a demonstrated talent for working with larger accounts. Carolyn knew she needed to acknowledge and nurture Molly's skills in this area.

With Deirdre, Jonah, and even Aaron for that matter, she saw little difference in their responsibilities or skills.

Jonah. Complicated Jonah. Some months he throws himself into the job; at other times he seems uninterested. He spends too much time in Carolyn's office discussing minor problems that overwhelm and distract him. Several times a year, he hovers near being put on probation for underperforming.

Deirdre understands her job and gets it done. She appreciates and enjoys the freedom and income that accompany the profession of sales. Goal oriented, she knows how much she wants to earn and the steps needed to make it happen. She keeps slightly apart from the group.

Young, but with solid experience, Aaron has real potential. If Carolyn could work around the solutions consultant debacle, she felt certain he could mature into a strong producer. But he needs to be a teammate and earn the trust of his customers first.

After completing this exercise, Carolyn sees the reps less as a sales staff and more as individual contributors with distinct challenges and talent sets.

## Create a plan

Times change. What was once considered contemporary becomes stodgy or outdated. Sales related titles include:

- Area sales manager.
- Channel partner sales executive.
- Enterprise sales representative.

A difference exists, though, between progressive and confusing. Managers grappling with the issue of titles need to:

- Review and update the job descriptions. Even those only a few years old may no longer adequately describe the responsibilities of the position.
- Consider giving some reps a secondary designation like "new hire training coordinator" to complement their primary title.

## Job descriptions

Some sales leaders manage 30 or more reps whereas others supervise just a few. Others supervise a combination of seven field reps, four inside reps, and two reps calling exclusively on the transportation industry.

Create a specific job description for each type of rep on your staff. The director of sales in this scenario manages five reps: four field salespeople and one potentially calling on larger accounts. She needs to update the sales representative's job description and create one for the new, yet-to-be named position.

## Sample job description:
### Sales representative

Achieve sales goals assigned by company through calling on and increasing business with current clients in assigned geographic territory, sourcing new sales opportunities, and closing sales.

### Responsibilities:
### Reporting

- Report to the director of sales

### Territory

- Cover geographic territory/assigned accounts
- Follow call plan generated by territory planning software
- Conduct pre-call research to understand prospect/ client needs
- Prospect for new business
- Follow up on system-generated leads
- Resolve customer complaints and problems
- Generate proposals using approved templates

### CRM

- Input sales data and notes in CRM system
- Submit required sales reports on due dates

### Meetings

- Attend all sales staff and other required company meetings
- Participate in sales and product training
- Be present at assigned tradeshows and conventions
- Maintain professional and technical knowledge
- Monitor the competition by collecting current information

## Secondary designations

Clients often discuss a similar dilemma with me. They manage reps who:

- Act as a liaison between engineering and the customer.
- Primarily call on existing accounts.
- Have worked for the company a long time.
- Help train new hires during orientation.
- Focus on a handful of high-volume customers.

They want to acknowledge these individuals' unique contributions, but worry about altering the focus of their job: sales representative. I suggest adding a secondary business card designation that appears underneath the title of salesperson.

Company XYZ
Brad Salesperson
Senior Sales Representative
New Hire Training Coordinator
Phone: 999-999-9999
Mobile: 999-999-9999
Brad.salesperson@CompanyXYZ.com
*www.companyxyz.com*

At first, most resist the idea. Some ask questions like, "What's the big deal? Why would they get excited about that?" Others wonder if they'll be seen as showing favoritism. Although I understand their hesitations, I know these designations make a *big difference* to the reps.

Look for situations in which the reps fill unique roles within the company. Don't assign one to every rep. It takes away the uniqueness of the designation. Some reps won't want one. Others really haven't earned it.

As an example, sales leaders wanting to recognize reps with long tenures might decide to give all those with more than 10 years of service the title of senior sales representative.

To that end, the manager makes the following decisions:

| Rep | Previous Title | New Title | Designation |
|---|---|---|---|
| Brad | Sales Representative | Senior Sales Representative | New Hire Training Coordinator |
| Molly | Sales Representative | Sales Representative | Major Accounts Representative |
| Jonah | Sales Representative | Sales Representative | n/a |
| Deirdre | Sales Representative | Senior Sales Representative | n/a |
| Aaron | Sales Representative | Sales Representative | n/a |

# Major accounts

Larger accounts operate and expect to be treated differently. Not every rep wants to call on them. Those who do have the skills to:

- Deal with a longer sales cycle.
- Learn the accounts' buying process.
- Ask effective questions.
- Understand the difference between decision-makers and influencers.
- Build consensus.
- Identify and work with detractors.

Some reps call on the larger accounts in their assigned territory alongside accounts of all sizes. They make regular visits to the client. No major problems exist, but the larger accounts buy a fraction of what they could purchase. Sales remain stagnant.

Quick tip: If you manage someone who has the skills to work with larger accounts, it might be time to move a few out of the regular territories. Assign them to reps with the ability to maximize sales within a larger organization.

## Present the plan to executives

A sales leader has two issues here:
- Making all titles consistent within the sales organization
- Offering secondary designations to qualified reps

You may or may not have full authority over titles for the reps in your department. Either way, discuss the situation with your supervisor. Start a conversation about titles in general and the need to change, update, and amend them from time to time. Mention company growth and generational differences. Present your ideas for formalizing and handling the matter.

Your boss might have looked askance at the whole solutions consultant issue. Maybe he had no involvement at all. Walk him through your thought process behind wanting to give it a try and why you believe it didn't work out.

Outline your ideas on:
- Giving reps secondary designations like major accounts or new hire training coordinator.
- Reassigning some of the larger accounts to the new major accounts rep.
- Giving all reps with more than 10 years' experience the designation of senior sales representative.

Several of the changes you want to make involve sales policies and procedures. Get on the same page with your boss before you proceed.

## Address the issue with the rep

Speak with the solutions consultant first. Ask questions about why he wanted the title to begin with. He provided a cursory explanation during the interview. You know him better now. Dig a little deeper.

Some reps feel a sense of self-consciousness about being in the sales profession—even those with the talent and skills for the job. They might have been brought up to see sales as a less than honorable profession or moved into sales from another role. A vague title allows them to sell without being seen as a salesperson.

Review what has occurred, because since you hired him and agreed to the title:

- Several customers expressed confusion about his role at the company.
- His teammates are puzzled too.

Let him know you've made a decision to give all reps working for the company the title of sales representative. Explain your reasoning from both a company and a customer vantage point.

Own your part in this. Talk about agreeing to the title with the best of intentions. You wanted him to feel comfortable and the company to be seen as progressive. It simply hasn't worked out the way everyone thought it would.

Reps in this situation sometimes argue intensely about keeping their title. Others understand the situation and agree to the change. Stand your ground. Reiterate the decision as being in the company's best interests.

## Major accounts

In this case, the employee's request has merit. She didn't ask for an unorthodox title, just one that overstates the requested promotion. Avoid repeating your solutions consultant error. Don't agree to another title that isn't quite right, causes resentment, and confuses people.

Begin the discussion by talking about the importance of appropriateness and clarity of titles for the company, coworkers and, most significantly, the customer. Acknowledge her talents with large accounts. Let her know you want to expand her responsibilities in that area.

Tell her about your decision to give all reps the title of salesperson, with certain reps receiving secondary designations. Offer her the designation of major accounts.

Say something like, "In reviewing the customer list, I came to the conclusion that we really don't have national accounts. We do, however, have seven accounts of significance to the company. We think you're the best fit for handling these accounts."

Review the list of clients. Listen to her thoughts. The rep might negotiate with you on a few. Be open to hearing her views, then get back with her on a final decision.

## Major accounts: the other reps involved

With the changes, each salesperson stands to lose a large account or two in their territory, something no reps welcome. Position this as a decision made to foster company growth. Be ready with sales figures and a chart to back up your decision.

Explain that although they have done an adequate job of managing these accounts, growth has been stagnant. Illustrate the difference between current sales revenue and an account's potential. Give that a chance to sink in.

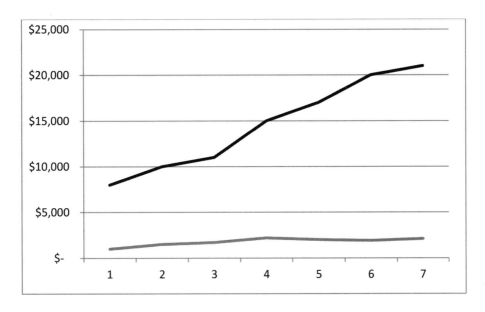

Some reps find the decision unfair. Others promise to work harder and expand their footprint within the account. Remind them they've had years, in some cases, to increase business. You've made the decision to create a major accounts role and this customer becomes part of that rep's responsibilities.

## One-on-one discussions

Decisions about titles affect all the reps in one way or another. Speak with each one individually, prior to making any announcements at a staff meeting. Be open to their thoughts and opinions.

## Current staff

Overall, these title changes represent positive moves forward for the company. In a staff meeting, announce plans to create:

- Standardized titles.
- Secondary designations.

Make a big deal out of this. Invite the president. Ask a few other executives who work closely with sales to attend. Give a brief speech acknowledging the two newly created positions of major accounts and new hire training coordinator as well as the senior sales designation.

> Quick tip: Publicly acknowledging promotions shows the staff the company recognizes individual talents and contributions and promotes from within.

## Hiring

Be clear with future applicants about titles and job descriptions. If a candidate requests an unusual title, politely decline. Explain your reasoning from the company perspective.

During the interview process, provide them with the job descriptions for the various sales positions at your organization. They'll gain a better understanding about the job they're being hired for and future opportunities within the department.

## New hire orientation

As new hires work with different reps during their training period, ask those with special designations to discuss their roles. Encourage them to talk to the new reps about their background and experience.

This gives new hires a great feeling about the organization. Those with ambitions beyond the position of sales rep see a career path versus a job.

## Leadership opportunities

Hot trends influence all of us on occasion. We get surprised by and agree to requests without fully thinking things through. It happens. How we go about extricating ourselves from these situations matters.

Reassigning titles, transferring accounts, and promoting employees involve a variety of skill sets. These decisions need to take place without moving away from the company's mission and core values. The ability to handle these situations shows strength, vision, tact, and diplomacy.

# Summary checklist
## Trouble with titles review and checklist

- Clarify problem.
- Review reps' individual contributions.
- Consider requests.
- Update:
  - Job descriptions
  - Titles
  - Account assignments
- Discuss with direct supervisor.
- Speak with the reps.
- Announce changes to the staff.

# Resolution

Aaron majored in engineering in college, but knew early on he didn't want to pursue it as a career. Earning good money, traveling, and working with a technical product appealed to him, but being called a sales rep did not. His college friends kidded him about going over to the dark side. One called him a sales weasel.

During several one-on-one meetings, he and Carolyn talked about what it meant to be in sales. He began to see it as a profession—one absolutely critical to the success of a company. His engineering friends might kid him, but he knows they couldn't succeed as reps because most don't have the social skills.

He now understands the importance of titles and has promised Carolyn to be a better teammate. She knows he works well with the engineering staff, and tells him she would consider the designation of engineering coordinator in the future.

Deirdre put up a fight to stop her largest account from being transferred to Molly. After a serious discussion about the account's potential, Carolyn relented and allowed her to keep it after Deirdre agreed to specific growth objectives. Deirdre understands she must meet those objectives this year or she will lose the account. Molly accepted the decision.

Carolyn underestimated how much designations mean to reps. She announced the various changes during a staff meeting, leaving Brad for last. She thanked him for his 20 years of service and his help with the new sales hires.

The president presented him with new business cards, a plaque, and a gift certificate to his favorite restaurant. The IT department changed his title (along with the others) on the Website. Carolyn put it up on the screen. He received a standing ovation from the group—and hasn't stopped smiling since.

# Chapter 6
# CRM Non-Compliance

Anxious for an update on XXText Inc., sales manager Mary reviews the account in the CRM system. Seeing Rick's entry, *7/14 3:14 p.m. spoke w/Abigail*, makes her wonder why she bothered. At least this message beats the typical entry: *SEM*. Translation: sent e-mail. Shortly after hiring him, Mary learned that if Rick entered any information into the CRM system *at all*, he used his own custom shorthand.

She knows he follows up on all his leads because his numbers reflect the effort. But he doesn't record the activity in the system. This leaves both Mary and the director of marketing frustrated.

Clients enjoy working with Rick. A solid performer so far, he's on track to surpass his third quarter sales quota by 15 percent. As his product knowledge increases, Mary only sees him improving. With salespeople being difficult to hire and retain, she hesitates to mention the CRM issue. She knows Rick finds the discussion petty and boring.

Unfortunately, the skimpy data leaves her uncertain about his potential sales. This forces her to spend time tracking him down for yet another translation.

Dave (the president and her boss) as well as other executives look at and complain about the notes and reports. Mary knows she loses credibility when they read the lame entries submitted by the salespeople. She wishes she had an answer.

---

### Problem Summary

Sales reps

- Input sloppy, incomplete, or no information
- Underutilize the CRM system
- Give appearance of not following up on leads

Sales manager has not

- Put a policy in place for substandard compliance
- Held reps accountable
- Created a CRM training manual
- Incorporated CRM training into new hire orientation

Executives

- Lose visibility into the business
- Complain about the situation
- Blame the sales manager

---

Mary *should* be concerned about careless or non-existent usage of the CRM system. The quality of the data logged by the reps reflects *directly* on her. Fair? Yes. She's the sales manager and being paid to run the sales department.

Information in the notes and the reports sections affects other departments outside of sales. The content influences decisions made within the company—a crucial factor in the organization's success.

As CEO, Dave needs accurate data on important accounts. Reading through the scant information provided, he has a right to ask, "Does Mary manage this group or are they managing her? Why can't she get them to leave decent notes?"

The CFO deciphering an inaccurate pipeline report might make critical errors in estimating cash flow and sales revenues for a given quarter. She will wonder, "Why does Mary allow this to go on month after month? She must know the reps have clogged and wildly optimistic pipelines!"

The marketing VP, uncertain which leads are the most productive, which competitors he faces, and under which circumstances, finds it difficult to help sales as much as he could. He might ask, "Are the lead gen programs even necessary?"

## Getting started

Sales managers in this situation should begin with notes. Though legitimate complaints about other sections abound (pipeline reports, lead follow-up), notes tend to be more obvious, read by the most people, and easiest to reach agreement on.

Hold back on addressing the sales staff about their CRM shortcomings. As the sales leader, determine for *yourself* what constitutes an acceptable, quality note. Read through some of the reps' worst notes. Ask yourself what makes a note unhelpful or useless. What type of additional information needs to be included? Why?

Next, read the notes of the salesperson in the organization doing the best job. What does this rep include in his notes that other reps skip? Which data adds value? Why? How do these detailed, accurate notes increase the salesperson's effectiveness?

Comparing poorly versus well-written notes provides a point of contrast. This enables you to recreate the most common sales scenarios and write best practice sample notes for each.

> Quick tip: For the best examples, look to your inside sales reps. At their computer all day, they typically use the CRM system more regularly and thoroughly.

# Create a plan

Take examples of inadequate CRM notes and edit the entries to reflect the type of information you and others at the company would benefit from seeing.

## Example #1

### Original Version

| Date | Time | Comments | Contact | Salesperson |
|------|------|----------|---------|-------------|
| 1-Jun | 9:42am | l/vm c/b | Abigail J | Rick |
| 3-Jun | 8:56am | l/vm c/b | Abigail J | Rick |
| 5-Jun | 10:29am | l/vm c/b | Abigail J | Rick |
| 9-Jun | 9:10am | l/vm c/b | Abigail J | Rick |

Purpose of call? Aways in the morning? What's being said? Have you discussed adding licenses before or will this be a new conversation?

### Improved Version

| Date | Time | Comments | Contact | Sales-person |
|------|------|----------|---------|--------------|
| 1-Jun | 9:42am | l/vm c/b | Abigail J | Rick |
| 3-Jun | 8:56am | l/vm c/b | Abigail J | Rick |
| 5-Jun | 10:29am | l/vm c/b | Abigail J | Rick |
| 9-Jun | 9:10am | left vm/sent email to Abigail. I want to set up an appt. to discuss aditional software licenses. She has asked to be called in the morning in past conversations. Having trouble getting through. | Abigail J | Rick |

Now mgr. and rep able to discuss adjusting v/m and email content as well as call times to better reach buyer.

## Example #2

| Date | Time | Comments | Contact | Salesperson |
|------|------|----------|---------|-------------|
| 10-Mar | 2:05pm | Lost deal | Aaron B | Donna |

To which competitor? For what reason? Where did we finish in the bidding process?

| Date | Time | Comments | Contact | Sales-person |
|------|------|----------|---------|--------------|
| 10-Mar | 2:05pm | Followed up with Aaron on bid proposal. Went with LPI, Inc. LPI charging $29.98 a cubic yard plus free delivery. Lost on delivery again. Logged in forecast report. | Aaron B | Donna |

Clear price and delivery problem recognized. Rep got hard facts. Meetings can take place re: pricing strateies offering additional benefits.

Either start or add this to the company sales toolkit (notebook containing examples of scripts, template e-mails, and common objections).

## Present the plan to executives

Let your direct supervisor know you want to address CRM compliance issues, beginning with the notes section. Explain why. Mention your desire to involve the executive team and your concern about team members insisting on tackling multiple CRM compliance issues all at once. Let him know you feel that will take the project offtrack as well as confuse and overwhelm the sales staff.

Enlist your boss' support. Provide assurances that after addressing the notes issue you plan to move on to the CRM issues bothering others in the company.

## Stand firm

Meet with those executives relying most heavily on the CRM. Clarify how you'd like to proceed by saying something like:

"I know you all have very justifiable complaints around CRM compliance. You find the sloppy and incomplete information as frustrating as I do. More than anything, I'd like to solve this problem. It affects everyone in the company. But I need support. In my experience, of all the CRM complaints, notes pop up most frequently. I want to deal with those first and then start improving other areas."

"I am putting together a CRM guide starting with notes. I take an example of an incomplete note, then edit it to include the type of information we all need to see. I want to use this document for tenured reps and new hires. If you would look the document over and give me your comments I'd appreciate it."

"For at least six weeks, I want to focus on notes exclusively. Once we all agree the frequency and quality of the notes has vastly improved, I'll start acting on other improvements you'd like to see. We could prioritize the list."

Gestures like accepting responsibility and listening to others' concerns help break down walls and engender cooperation with your coworkers.

## Address the issue with the rep

Prior to meeting with the reps individually, speak to the sales staff as a group first. I advise addressing the entire team initially, because almost every sales staff member could probably improve their CRM usage on some level.

Begin the CRM notes discussion toward the end of a routine staff meeting. If some or all of the reps work remotely or times zones present an issue, have them participate via conference call or Skype. Make every effort so the sales staff hears the *same message at the same time*.

Avoid pointing fingers or sounding negative. Emphasize *company* needs and the importance of improved CRM information. Save praise or constructive criticism for one-on-one meetings.

Set the tone with some introductory remarks along the lines of, "As a company, everyone from our president to the VP of marketing relies on information put into the CRM system. We need to improve the quality of that data. I will be e-mailing all of you a document showing samples of typical notes and examples of notes with better, more helpful information.

"Before discussing this as a group, I'd like all of you to look the document over. I'll be setting up times for us to review this one-on-one."

## Table a discussion

Why *not* talk about the notes document during the meeting? Everyone's there, right? The problem is that every rep uses the system differently. For instance, all sales staffs have a CRM guru—the one who enjoys fully utilizing the whole system. They know it backward and forward, reveling in creating reports just for themselves. Most sales staffs have one person who never uses the system at all. Then we have the vast majority of reps who do the minimum.

As their manager, you have varying compliments, critiques, or suggestions for different reps. Deal with each one based on their individual level of CRM participation:

- Consistent users flat-out resent wasting time on such a discussion.
- Reps underutilizing the system fear being called out.
- Gurus sometimes dominate the conversation.

Technologically, not all reps get on board at the same time and level. One or two may never join the party.

## One-on-one meetings

Start each meeting with a recap of what you said in the staff meeting. Re-emphasize group and company. Begin the conversation with a series of questions such as:

- What were your thoughts on the notes document?
- As a sales staff, what grade would you give us for CRM usage?
- What do you think about your own notes?

Listen to their responses. You might learn a few things you didn't know and view their note leaving system in a different light.

Most importantly, customize the chat. Prepare a document with samples of the reps' notes—some of good quality and some in need of improvement. Start with a strong note and say something like, "When I read this, it really helped me out. I know that you were making progress with the client and then she just stopped returning your calls."

Examples need not be limited to actual notes in the system. When reps leave notes only sporadically, mention that. "You've done a good job increasing business with Wordsource over the last few years. You see or call them regularly. It just never gets reflected in the notes. Months go by without a single entry. If you ever have problems there or need support for a presentation, I won't know about it. If you were the sales manager, what would you want to see?"

## Work together

Between the document and the one-on-one conversations about their individual notes styles, the reps sense a change. Don't let up; keep the momentum going. Pick a day for each rep. Ask them not to put notes in the system after each call. Request, instead, that they type notes into a file and save it.

If the salespeople (like an inside salesperson) make many, many calls per day, typing them all into a separate document would be too burdensome. Have them record half a dozen or so. Field reps typically go on less than half a dozen calls a day, so have them record all of their calls for that day in a separate document.

On the appointed day, pull up a chair at the reps' desk, cubicle, or office. Talk through the notes they wrote down. With thorough and helpful notes, offer compliments. In the case of incomplete notes, point out additions to improve the quality. Enter the notes into the CRM system together.

For remote reps, conduct this activity over the phone. Have them e-mail a file to you. Talk through the note-entering process in the same way as with the other reps. Use a screen-sharing app so that you can both view what's being entered.

# Seriously?

Those reading this book might be screeching at this very moment, "You're kidding, right? Ask the reps to record their notes on a piece of paper, and then sit next to them and discuss the notes? Is she crazy? This would be embarrassing for me and the reps. We're all adults. It's part of their job. Plus, I don't have time for this."

Yes, I'm recommending you sit right next to the reps as they put notes in the system. Yes, you're all adults. Yes, it's part of the reps' job. But guess what? These *adults* aren't leaving the quality or quantity of notes other employees need to see to effectively understand what's going on with the accounts at any given time.

Managers need to steel themselves for the awkwardness of the situation—the covert eye rolling and intra-team texting on the part of the reps. It goes with the territory. Leaders demonstrate proper methodology. They mentor, correct mistakes, review progress, acknowledge improvement, and hold people accountable. That's their role.

# Avoid a solo effort

Integrate the other executives into the notes project at this point. Have them meet or speak periodically with the reps. They agreed to help you, remember? Ask them to compliment as often as possible, not just critique. They should be specific about what they want to see and read. As I keep stressing, they have a stake in this CRM issue, too.

Imagine the impact if the marketing VP picks up the phone and thanks a rep for their detailed notes on a lead they followed up with. Think about reps' reactions to the product manager e-mailing a rep and requesting additional information on an important client.

Most sales professionals possess some empathy. They need it as they listen to customers and prospects, ask questions, address objections, and close deals. When others take the time to explain why detailed, comprehensible CRM information helps them do their job more effectively, it will motivate them to leave higher quality notes.

# Continued vigilance

Assistance and participation from others in the company help any manager trying to enact change. But the overall success of this project hinges on one thing: your consistent monitoring of the notes of each rep. If reps log quick, unhelpful entries or fail to enter one at all, the manager needs to have a conversation with them *as soon as possible.*

When Rick leaves another *l v/m wcb* note, Mary needs to communicate with him about that *right away.* She should pick up the phone and say, "Rick, please include more detail on your recent XXText Inc. notes entry by the end of today."

> Quick tip: Most CRM systems allow interested parties (executives, etc.) to "watch" selected accounts, getting updates when a rep modifies the account. Encourage executives to watch accounts that interest them. This reminds reps that people review what they enter.

## Still a problem?

What do you do when one of your salespeople simply will not record information in the CRM system on a regular basis? You need to take action. I recommend approaching the problem from several different angles.

## Job description

Amend current job descriptions to include specific information about CRM expectations. Use the document to support you, both during the interview process and later on, for dealing with a rep in non-compliance. Have candidates for open sales positions read the job description at some point during the interview process.

## Performance reviews

Include CRM compliance in the document as part of the review. Accurately assess a rep's usage of the system. Many times other executives sign these reviews. With non- or inconsistent CRM users, seeing negative comments in writing and knowing those comments will most likely be seen by others gives most of them pause to think.

# Bonuses

Companies using a base salary and commission plan only, miss the mark in my opinion. Bonuses allow organizations to recognize and pay for other behaviors such as: participation in staff meetings and training, appropriate treatment of company property, sales reports turned in on a timely basis and, yes, CRM compliance.

Hold back a small percentage of the money paid out in commission to create a bonus program. Money missed due to sloppiness or lack of discipline, to many reps, feels like money given away. That makes an impression.

# Future opportunities

Some talented salespeople covet eventual promotions to positions such as national account rep or sales manager. Entering detailed, precise information into the sales software program or managing those who do becomes critical in these upper level roles.

During performance reviews or career related talks, communicate that their candidacy for any of those positions would be seriously questioned. They've never demonstrated consistent CRM habits. How could they be relied upon to do so with important large accounts or when overseeing other sales reps? Being told that an issue as *fixable* as CRM compliance disqualifies them for future promotions comes as sobering news for the majority of reps.

# Vigilant management

Most companies tolerate top-performing, non-CRM complying reps. Sourcing, hiring, and training reps prove such a difficult and expensive undertaking, most won't risk terminating them for this issue.

With certain reps, nothing does the trick—not lectures, critical performance reviews, or lower bonuses. Managers unwilling to put this rep on probation or terminate their employment must babysit versus manage. No other alternative exists.

Periodically sit next to them and enter the data together. Call or text the moment you read a poorly written note. Alert them when weeks have gone by without a note on a particular company. Wearying, inefficient, frustrating, tiring—you bet. Getting accurate data from this rep—critical. Letting them get away with non-compliance—out of the question.

If you know you'll never put them on probation (at least for the CRM issue) you have to be willing to do it.

> Quick tip: In a team selling environment, have an inside rep enter data on behalf of a field rep who debriefs them by phone about a customer visit. Field reps have plenty of behind the wheel time. Make the most of it.

# Hiring

Before hiring another new sales rep, incorporate questions about CRM compliance into the interview process. Include questions such as:

- How do you view the role of CRM in the sales effort?
- What constitutes a good note?
- Apart from notes, which CRM function do you use frequently?
- Explain your lead generation follow-up system.

For subsequent interviews, ask them to show you examples of their notes for a current client.

# New hire orientation

Experienced leaders know new hires copy the behavior they see exhibited by the current reps.

Eager to succeed, new reps diligently enter detailed information into the software. After a few months, they realize *no other rep* seems to put the same amount of effort in. In fact, one barely uses the system at all.

With time, these salespeople cease to be the new guy. Other reps join the company and suddenly they have a little seniority. Pretty soon, they stop paying as much attention to CRM compliance. They don't stop altogether, but they get sloppy sometimes. Hey, they're making their numbers. In fact, they're outperforming a few of the more tenured reps. What's the big deal?

Don't allow this to happen. Take precautions to support all your hard work in this area by having CRM training play a big role during new hire orientation.

Ask the new employee to read through documented CRM examples, and then send you notes from their first few sales calls. Together, put those notes in the CRM system. Compliment them when they include helpful details. Offer advice about leaving more effective information for yourself and other employees. Communicate with them immediately if you see they've left an incomplete note.

As they rotate through different departments during the first few weeks, make sure other employees include CRM discussions as part of the training process. Keep CRM compliance/best practices at the forefront.

## Leadership opportunities

CRM compliance represents a vicious cycle for a lot of sales executives. Others in the company point the finger at them for slap dash or nonexistent data input from the sales staff. They get on the reps for a period of time and a slight improvement occurs—temporarily. Distracted with other deals, sales managers pay less attention, the quality of notes deteriorates, and the cycle begins again.

Mary took responsibility, did her homework, drafted a plan, and presented a time table to those in the organization using and most affected by the CRM. She explained the how's and why's of what she was trying to accomplish and listened to others' opinions.

Actions like these allow a manager to ask not for help but for *support* from others. There's a big difference. She looked like a strong and capable leader, because she *took the lead* on this project.

## Summary checklist
### CRM non-compliance review and checklist

- Clarify problem.
- Outline strategy.
- Create documentation.
- Involve executives and other employees.
- Retrain current staff.
- Work with non-compliant reps.
- Retool:
  - Job description

- New hire orientation
- Performance reviews
- Bonus plan
- Propose next CRM initiative.

# Resolution

Looking at her phone, Mary sees a text from Rick asking her to read his latest CRM entry for XXText Inc. He says he sincerely hopes he's provided enough detail. In the notes for yesterday, she sees the following:

"Meeting with Abigail went well. We laughed because we both wore blue suits. But she had on a white shirt while mine was light blue with a maroon stripe. She offered me a cup of coffee but I said no. The coffee at XXText always has a chemical taste to it (though I did not tell her that). She apologized for the number of times I had to call her to set this appointment up. XXText changed their policy about licenses. They want to create a committee to review all licenses 2x a year. Abigail would like to be on that committee, but doesn't know if she'll be appointed. Her overall thoughts on our software are positive, though. She has no interest in switching vendors. I will call her in 2 weeks to find out about the committee and the extra licenses. It was raining when I arrived at XXText, but the sun was out when I left. I grabbed a quick sandwich for lunch."

Mary smiled. After all that she had been through with CRM compliance, things had begun to turn around. She e-mailed the VP of marketing and told him to read it. Not known for his humor, even he thought it was funny.

Rick's message, though facetious, demonstrates his understanding of what she was asking for in the notes section. A new respect exists between the sales reps and other executives at the company when it comes to the importance of entering accurate, concise, and relevant data. Communication between all parties has improved.

On her end, Mary schedules certain times during the day to review reps' notes. When one falls below the newly set standards, she doesn't throw up her hands or send a text. She calls the rep and discusses it directly. She asked for, and has received, consistent support from her boss and the VP of marketing. The CFO remains a work in progress.

Four weeks into the agreed-upon six weeks for the notes project, Mary met with the other executives to prioritize a list of new CRM compliance initiatives. As a group, they agreed upon which module to address next.

She sent Rick a quick text asking him what kind of sandwich he ordered for lunch. His text read Italian panini—excellent.

# Chapter 7
# The Mysterious Remote Salesperson

Vice president of sales Sharon wanted a dedicated field salesperson, not manufacturers' reps and distributors, calling on the company's customers in certain geographic areas. Finally, her boss approved and put the position in the budget. The salesperson she hired, Jan, would live and work on the West Coast, flying to the home office in the Midwest once a quarter.

At first, everything seemed fine. Having prior industry experience, Jan learned the products quickly. CRM notes indicated she called on her assigned accounts regularly. She was always available to video conference or chat on the phone when people at the home office needed to speak with her.

After a few months, things began to change. Jan's dedicated customer service representative (CSR) mentioned how difficult it had become to reach her. Sharon spoke to Jan about it. She offered plausible explanations for everything—early morning sales calls, presentations running late, a sick day, and taking clients out to lunch.

Sharon relayed Jan's explanations to the CSR, confidently and enthusiastically adding, "We've never worked with a remote rep before. We just have to be more flexible about communicating with her."

Jan had experience working remotely and had come highly recommended. Having advocated for hiring a field rep, Sharon wanted to see Jan succeed.

Sharon scheduled a video conference with Jan. She placed the call, but Jan didn't connect, nor did she make any attempt to reach Sharon the rest of the day. When Sharon called Jan's cell phone, voice mail answered.

---

### **Problem Summary**

Sales rep
- Hired to cover geographic territory
- Worked in a remote capacity previously
- Initially easy to reach and communicate with
- Suddenly difficult to get in touch with; misses meetings

Vice president of sales
- Fought to hire a dedicated remote salesperson
- Enjoyed good rapport with the rep at the beginning
- Hears complaints about the rep being hard to reach

---

## Questioning reps' work habits/honesty

Decades ago, only large companies (such as pharmaceutical, consumer products, and machinery) had the ability to deploy a direct, remote sales force. These organizations hired regional sales managers to supervise six or more field reps covering an assigned geographic territory.

These reps spoke with their regional sales manager on the phone regularly and turned in a variety of reports. Managers flew out or drove to meet with the reps and accompany them on sales calls. Riding in the car between appointments, they asked questions of and coached the reps on particular deals and better sales techniques.

If a problem arose with a rep, the regional sales manager took it up with the rep, the VP of sales, and human resources. Corrective action was taken, up to and including termination of the salesperson.

Companies with remote sales forces also employed customer service staffs who took calls from the reps, dealt with any order problems, and answered questions that might come up. Shipping departments mailed boxes of brochures, samples, and office supplies to the homes of the field sales staff. Entire systems of checks and balances existed to keep track of the rep and help them do their job.

Smaller companies lacking the infrastructure to employ a field sales force have two options: manufacturers' reps or distribution companies. In order to make a living, the manufacturers' reps have to represent several non-competing products from a variety of companies. Larger distributors might carry hundreds of products from a variety of organizations. Though better than no coverage at all, this means companies don't have the manufacturer's rep or distributors' complete focus on their product.

Technology enables companies of all sizes to hire remote reps for either inside phone sales or field coverage in areas of the country they never thought possible. An employee of the organization, these salespeople represent only the employer's goods and services.

Although all companies now have the capability to hire remotely, many still lack the infrastructure to support the rep. Most still operate largely unmanaged. This leads to problems.

## Getting started

In my consulting work with companies, two subjects make for the most awkward conversations with clients: the unqualified VP of sales (Chapter 14) and the mysterious remote rep. When discussing the remote rep, most of the conversations start off with phrases like:

- "I just don't know what they're doing all day."
- "They could have called through their account list three times by now, but they've only made their way through a third of the list."
- "I can't quite figure them out."

For this problem, getting *started* involves starting to *get real* about the situation. This rep most likely has a second job or an obligation of some sort they didn't disclose during the interview process or that developed after working for you.

When I suggest this to clients, I meet with (usually in order) denial, resistance, and anger. I am told that:

- Under no circumstance would this rep do anything underhanded.
- They've been in the industry for years and enjoy a stellar reputation.
- A respected colleague personally recommended them.
- I have a lot of nerve even to suggest such a thing.

Based on my experience with this issue, the possibilities include:

- A second job.
- Addiction.
- Debt.
- Health issues.
- Domestic problems.
- An intrusive hobby.

The remote rep's second job or other involvement may not compete directly with the position you hired them for. But it does prevent them from devoting full time and attention to their responsibilities within the work day.

## Uncover the pattern

Most of my clients facing this issue calm down a few days after our initial conversation and listen to my advice. I tell them to "Look for the pattern. This person does or does not do something on a regular, repetitive basis. You have to uncover it." They assure me that no pattern exists, but agree to look into it to satisfy me.

I recommend running reports showing: CRM activity, computer login times, e-mailing times, phone calls placed or missed, customer visits, and so on. Be sure to make the adjustment to their local time zone in considering your observations.

| Date | Time | Contact | Result |
|------|------|---------|--------|
| 7-Jul | 8:00am | | |
| 7-Jul | 9:00am | | |
| 7-Jul | 10:00am | | |
| 7-Jul | 11:32am | Sam | email sent |
| 7-Jul | 11:40am | Darla | left voice mail |
| 7-Jul | 11:53am | Kent | Receptionist said on vaca all week. Back 7/16 |
| 7-Jul | 1:10pm | Angie | set appointment for 8/3 |
| 7-Jul | 2:00pm | Jerry | spoke about product; not interested |
| 7-Jul | 3:00pm | Leo | set appointment for 8/5 |
| 7-Jul | 4:00pm | | |
| 7-Jul | 5:00pm | | |

| Date | Time | Contact | Result |
|------|------|---------|--------|
| 9-Jul | 8:00am | | |
| 9-Jul | 9:00am | | |
| 9-Jul | 10:00am | | |
| 9-Jul | 11:02am | Martin | left v/m |
| 9-Jul | 11:13am | Abbie | email sent |
| 9-Jul | 11:40am | Paul | left v/m |
| 9-Jul | 2:34pm | Don | sales call; interested in current promotion |
| 9-Jul | 3:00pm | Johanna | set appointment for 7/29 |
| 9-Jul | 4:00pm | | |
| 9-Jul | 5:00pm | | |

All clients come back to me and say the exact same thing: "You were right. She doesn't log into the computer on Tuesdays and Thursdays until 11:00 a.m." Or "He virtually disappears from 12:00 p.m. to 2:30 p.m. several days a week. He never answers his cell or responds to e-mails or texts."

## Check in with customers

Remote or local, once a new rep begins meeting with customers, sales leaders should follow up with a few of them. This activity takes on greater importance if you rarely or never work with reps in the field. So many problems could be uncovered early on if sales leaders did this with regularity.

When selecting customers to call, I recommend reading through the CRM notes looking for a certain type of information. Contact accounts where the remote rep indicates:

- Visiting several times
- Leaving multiple voice-mail messages
- Sending numerous e-mails

During conversations with the accounts, do not in any way indicate suspicion or disappointment with the remote rep. Make the call about the customer and their satisfaction with the salesperson. Ask if the salesperson:

- Shows up on time for scheduled appointments.
- Comes prepared for the meeting.
- Conducts themselves professionally.
- Returns customers' calls.
- Gets back to them with answers to questions.
- Sends requested information.

After two or three calls, most sales leaders discover the rep has misrepresented their activity in the field. When they say they've visited a customer several times, the customer has seen them only once. If they claim to have left several voice mails, the customer has received only one or none.

## Account coverage

Sales leaders become concerned when, after a reasonable period of time has gone by, remote reps haven't spoken to or visited their entire customer list. They expect new reps to make at least initial contact with their assigned accounts as quickly as possible.

Between knowledge of these customers and territory coverage software, determine how much time it should take an inside rep to call through their customer list or a field rep to meet with all their accounts one-on-one.

> Quick tip: Other warning signs could include: insisting on using their own, not company provided, laptop, cell phone, fax machine, or other equipment; never turning in cell phone or other related bills; experiencing more IT problems than the average rep; and insisting on using local (not company) IT assistance.

## Productivity standards

Problems or suspicions with remote reps often emerge as early as six weeks and usually well before their first full business quarter with the company. That might not be enough time to see a discernible change in the revenue numbers one way or the other.

If you set graduated 30-, 60-, 90-day goals for activities like prospecting calls, e-mails, lead follow-up, presentations, and proposals, the remote rep should be ramping up and even starting to exceed those targets.

Look for signs of the remote reps not increasing activity much past the 30-day mark. Most, if they have another job or responsibilities, plateau between the 30- and 60-day productivity goals.

## Create a plan

As a first step, review all offer letters, employment contracts, as well as sales and company policies. Were these written before hiring a remote rep? Were clauses added for their special circumstances in working apart from the home office? If not, update any and all appropriate documents. Explicitly communicate expectations for the remote rep in contracts, offers of employment, and written policies.

## Sample employment offer

**Salary**

The starting base training salary for this position is $73,000, paid twice a month via auto-pay.

You will be eligible for commissions, bonuses, and earnings from sales contests as stated in the compensation plan.

**Benefits**

The company offers medical insurance and pays 50 percent of the cost. We offer a matching 401(k) plan and short-term disability. Employees become eligible for benefits 90 days after their start date.

Dental, vision, long-term disability, and life insurance are electives and available under a separate carrier.

Vacation allotment is 10 paid days per year. In addition, there are two paid personal days and five paid sick days annually.

**Attendance**

The company's office hours are 8:30 a.m. to 5:30 p.m., Monday through Friday.

Those salespeople working remotely must notify their direct supervisor and speak in-person with a manager in the home office if they need to call in sick or take an unscheduled personal day.

Vacation days must be requested in advance and receive approval of their direct supervisor.

Remote salespeople must be available for full-time work from 8:30 a.m. to 5:30 p.m. and be able to devote full attention to the company (answering calls, returning client calls, attending meetings, and making sales calls) during this time period.

**Territory**

In the position of sales representative, you have responsibility for all direct sales activity in the West Coast territory.

**Expenses**

On the first day of employment, you will be issued a laptop with company-approved software and cellular phone. All maintenance and related costs will be the responsibility of the company. We provide a car allowance of $395 per month. Repair and service work are the responsibility of the sales representative. Any additional work-related expenses will be reimbursed after an expense form is submitted.

A breach of these agreements could result in discipline up to and including termination.

## Gather the facts

When faced with this situation, keep a log to document conversations and observations. This organizes the information for discussions with supervisors, human resources, and the rep in question.

| Date | Conversation |
|---|---|
| 2-Jul | CSR mentions Jan has become difficult to reach. |
| 3-Jul | Spoke to Jan. She provided explanation of early morning sales calls, sick day, and appointments running late. |
| 5-Jul | Scheduled video conference with Jan. She did not show up for call. Made no contact with me all day long. |
| 7-Jul | Should be making 5 in-person calls per day. Making 2-3 on average. |
| 10-Jul | Ran activity report. Last three weeks, Tuesdays and Thursdays, Jan doesn't log in until 11am or later. |
| 12-Jul | Asked Jan about full workday availability. She assured me there were no problems. |
| 15-Jul | Second conversation. I bring up not logging in until 11am. She mentions multiple IT issues preventing her from logging in on time. I schedule a field visit with her. |
| 15-Jul | Rep does not log in the rest of the day. |
| 16-Jul | Rep does not log into system. No activity. |

Should you have to take the unfortunate step of putting the remote rep on warning, this exercise makes the facts easily accessible.

## Work with the rep

For a field rep, take a day or two out of your schedule and pay them a visit in their home territory. If your research has shown the remote rep rarely logs in before 11:30 a.m. on Tuesdays and Thursdays, fly out Monday evening and plan to accompany them on calls starting at 8:30 a.m. on a Tuesday morning.

This rep should be ready and prepared to work each day. You don't need to provide more than a few days' notice.

## Inside salesperson

In the case of a remote inside sales representative, make arrangements, with their full knowledge, to record their conversations with customers. Explain needing to monitor their calls to provide coaching and ensure they are staying in line with the company's best practices.

As with the field rep, schedule the recordings for those days they log in late or have several hours of unexplained inactivity.

---

Quick tip: Be sure to abide by all laws and regulations regarding the recording of calls including, but not limited to, notifying customers about their calls being recorded for training purposes.

---

## Present the plan to executives

When discussing this situation with a boss, you're really bringing up two entirely different topics with regard to remote reps:

- Dealing with a non-performer
- Creating a successful, repeatable hiring process for remote reps

No one enjoys acknowledging a plan they fought for didn't work out. Despite that, try to keep the conversation upbeat. Hiring a remote field rep works for all kinds of companies. Don't give up on this. Conduct some research beforehand. Talk about organizations similar in size to yours that successfully manage remote reps.

Begin with the most pressing problem—the remote rep's performance. Share your findings about their non-availability during the workday. Acknowledge not anticipating some of the difficulties you've experienced with her so far.

Listen to what your boss or others have to say. Some probably have previous experience dealing with a remote sales force and can offer solid advice on handling the situation. As a group, agree on the next steps to take.

Let your boss or the group know if things don't work out with the current rep; you want to hire again for that territory. Should you be able to get the problems with this salesperson under control, you would like approval to hire a remote rep for another territory.

Review your plan for managing future remote hires, including:

- Additional clauses on employment contracts.
- Background checks.
- Discussion of availability during stated company hours.
- Regular trips to work with the rep in their territory.
- Tighter 30-, 60-, 90-day goals.

End the meeting by thanking all the parties for their support. Agree to keep them informed about any discussions or new problems with the remote rep.

## Address the issue with the rep

During the first conversation ask them, "Would there be any reason you cannot work during the company's stated hours of Monday through Friday, 8:30 a.m. to 5:30 p.m.?" Let silence fall and see what they have to say.

In my experience, remote reps react in three different ways:

- Act insulted that you would even think to accuse them of not being completely available
- Answer in a very business-like manner that nothing prevents them from working the entire day
- Start talking a blue streak about sick days, computer issues, or getting tied up in traffic

Listen, but don't confront them. Have your log of infractions visible on your screen, only referencing them unless you have to—because you probably won't. Interestingly, reps in this situation rarely ask obvious questions such as, "Why would you ask?" or "Has something happened that we should talk about?"

In all likelihood, the salesperson accepted the position knowing they couldn't devote their full attention to it. Something or someone prevents them from doing so. After this initial conversation, they know two things: They can't keep this juggling act going forever, and you are on to them.

For now, leave it right there. You've made your point. Continue as normal with the rest of the call. Schedule a time to speak again within the next few days. Don't let a lot of time elapse between conversations.

## Be prepared

The majority of the time, remote reps let this situation play out until the company decides to terminate their employment. Once in a while, they think the situation over and decide to be candid.

Don't be surprised if your cell phone rings and they decide to talk. Often, they make statements like:

- I'm going through a divorce.
- My child support payments are in arrears.
- I have elder care issues with an aging parent.

People have problems—some quite complicated and stressful. If, as this person's manager, you think they have potential for success, say something like, "I really appreciate your leveling with me. Talk to me more specifically about the situation."

Start asking questions to determine:

- How long the situation has been going on.
- The time line needed to solve the problem.
- What type of support they need.

Work with your boss and human recourses to come up with a plan everyone can live with. Perhaps the rep could work three-quarters or part-time for a few months. Maybe a temporary four-day work week would help. Adjust their salary accordingly.

Set up a regular time to speak specifically about their situation. More importantly than anything else, agree to an end date. I would not recommend letting this situation go on for longer than 90 days.

## Follow-up conversation

Begin the second talk by saying, "When we spoke a few days ago, you assured me there was nothing preventing you from giving the company your full time and attention, Monday through Friday. Do I understand that correctly? Can you explain a few things?"

Ask questions along the lines of:

- Why does the CRM show no activity on Tuesdays and Thursdays until 11:30 a.m. or later?
- The buyer at iSTEM told me he's only met with you once. You have three in-person visits logged into the notes section. What's going on there?

Address everything they say directly. If they mention IT problems, set up a three-way conference call between you, the rep, and technical support. If traffic comes up, ask specific questions about the route they take. Details make mysterious remote reps very uncomfortable.

End the call by letting them know you'll be flying out to work with them on Tuesday of next week. You'll meet them in the hotel lobby at 7:30 a.m. sharp so the two of you can have breakfast together and discuss the upcoming account visits. Tell them that, going forward, if they experience any problem that prevents them from being on the phone or visiting a customer by 8:30 a.m., they should contact you directly and immediately.

## Anything could happen

Confronted and realizing they can't make this work anymore, some reps resign. Others literally disappear. You simply never hear from them again. They stop logging on to their computer or entering notes. Some wait to get put on warning and are ultimately terminated.

Regardless of which path the reps choose, if you see no improvement after the second conversation, put them on probation. Follow your company's standard policies and procedures for this process.

## Address the rest of the staff

Non-performance issues with any rep remain confidential. None of the other salespeople need to be involved in this situation. If you manage other remote reps, discuss any changes to employment contracts. Communicate with them about signing updated documents related to their job.

# Hiring

Before starting a search, make the appropriate changes to offer letters, employment contracts, and any other relevant documents.

When speaking with applicants who have worked remotely before, ask:

- Can you walk me through your process for communicating with your boss/home office?
- What meetings were you required to attend (remotely)? Did you use video conferencing or conference calling?
- How did you handle any customer problems that arose?
- What do you like best/worst about working remotely?
- When you feel unmotivated, how do you go about turning things around?
- What can we as a company do on our end to make this relationship work as smoothly as possible?

For applicants never having worked remotely before, ask:

- Have you ever known anyone who worked in a remote capacity from company headquarters before?
- What did they say about their experience?
- How do you structure your day currently?
- What do you think the most difficult part of working independently will be?

---

Quick tip: Have candidates take a pre-employment assessment before extending an offer. Among other attributes, it should indicate whether or not they have the ability to work independently.

---

David Sawyer, a professional with more than 35 years in the private security industry and president of Safer Places, Inc., a background screening firm, suggests using background checks, credit reports, database searches, and the IRS.

## Background check

Require a background check as part of the hiring process. The release form most new hires sign gives permission for as long as they remain an employee (this varies state by state).

## Credit reports

Ask your background screening company to run a credit report. Often, employers get listed near the top of this document.

## Database search

Many background screening firms outsource their employment verifications to other companies. A search of this database may show title and dates of employment. If the dates are current, you'll know they have a second job.

## The IRS

This agency is an excellent source for verifying salary and employers. However, they require a special release form to be signed for each search. Include this in your initial background check. Then consider making it a policy to run an annual background check and include the IRS search every year.

## New hire orientation

Most companies have remote reps visit the home office or headquarters for a week of orientation. Sales leaders introduce them to department leaders and other employees they'll work with frequently.

Right after that visit, the ball often gets dropped. During the first quarter, schedule follow-up conversations between remote reps and those they met at the home office. Don't leave it up to the rep and make these conversations mandatory.

Work with them, in their territory, once a month for several months in a row. Observe their:

- Interactions with customers.
- Sales style.
- Organizational skills.
- Product knowledge.

Leave time in between calls to offer help and coaching.

## Leadership opportunities

Many sales leaders have fought for, proposed, or presented ideas for a new initiative or project at some point in their career. Sometimes these initiatives fail, at least on the first pass. Don't give up. Get mad, feel disappointed, and then try again.

The remote rep was taking advantage of your company. Instead of doing nothing out of embarrassment, you faced the problem head-on. If you made some mistakes, acknowledge them. Get input from others about what they thought went wrong. Offer specific details about any additions or changes you recommend for the next remote rep.

Successfully hiring and managing remote salespeople increases your company's footprint in a given territory substantially. Making this work shows your abilities as a forward thinking and fearless groundbreaker.

## Summary checklist

### The mysterious remote rep review and checklist

- Clarify problem.
- Review:
  - Employment agreements
  - Offer letters
- Research remote rep's
  - CRM activity
  - Cell phone records
  - Login times
  - Performance against productivity
- Update employment contracts.

- Speak with the rep about
  - Unaccounted-for time during workday
  - Lack of activity
- Work with or put the rep on warning.

# Resolution

On Monday morning, Sharon took a deep breath before calling Jan. She wanted to remain calm and conduct the conversation professionally.

She began by asking Jan why she hadn't logged in prior to 11:30 a.m. last Thursday. Jan assured her she started her day at 8 a.m., but couldn't access the CRM system. Sharon said, "Tell me about that. What happened?"

Jan spoke for five minutes straight about the technology problems she had faced since joining the company. Sharon let her speak uninterrupted and then said, "Let's set up a video conference with Linda in technical support. We need to solve these issues so you can enter notes successfully."

After objecting strenuously, saying she'd figure it out on her own, Jan begrudgingly agreed to a time. Next, Sharon told her she'd be out to work with her on Thursday. Jan tried to talk her out of it, but Sharon held her ground. They selected a time and a place to meet.

For the rest of Monday and all day Tuesday, Jan did not log in to the system or add any notes to the CRM. On Wednesday morning she called Sharon and told her she had accepted a position with another company.

Though aggravated and disappointed, Sharon also realizes she did the right thing. Jan was not devoting her full time and attention to the company. Who really knew what she was doing out in the field? She might be saying or doing the wrong things and damaging the company's reputation. Despite the outcome, Sharon understands many of the mistakes she made and wants to try again.

# Chapter 8
# Unethical Behavior

To veteran sales manager Charles, sales contests always seemed slightly unpredictable. You never knew which reps would find these mini-competitions the most motivating. No two salespeople he had managed took them more seriously than Tyler and Stacey.

Both solid producers, they turned every contest into a two-person race. If the other reps won as well, then that was great. But the real prize for both was outdoing the other. They good-naturedly motivated themselves and everyone else on the team.

To boost revenues for the slowest month of the year (July), Charles created a contest: Any rep increasing their sales from July of the prior year by 10 percent won a $150 gift certificate at the local mall. The rep realizing the largest increase for July received a $250 gift certificate.

Reps not with the company the prior year had to beat the overall sales-person average for last July by 10 percent. Contest rules stated the company's software must be sold and installed on or before the last day of the contest.

Grand prize winner Tyler won not only the $250 gift certificate, but lunch at his favorite restaurant, courtesy of Stacey. That was the personal bet between them. Tyler, of course, let the whole office know.

While checking contest sales, Charles discovered that Tyler placed an order for a customer on the second to last day of July, and then put the order on hold on the last day of July. On the first day of August, he changed the installation date to October. Charles thought only CSRs had that ability, but the entry showed Tyler made the change. How had he managed to do it? His actions were in clear violation of the contest rules.

Charles felt surprised and disappointed. He had never had trouble of any kind with Tyler. To his knowledge, he had a spotless record. Had Tyler ever cheated before and just not gotten caught? Was Stacey in on this? Should he dismiss him immediately over $250? Was probation the solution? Who else knew about this?

---

### Problem summary

Sales rep
- Revels in sales contests
- Participates in a friendly rivalry with a teammate
- Enjoys a reputation as an ethical sales rep
- Falsified an order to win a recent sales contest

Sales manager
- Believes in the importance of sales contests
- Manages two very competitive reps
- Discovered one of those reps falsified an order to win
- Feels deceived and shaken by the situation

---

Cheating sometimes goes on within sales forces. When this occurs, sales leaders must take the matter seriously and deal with it directly.

A problem like this has always been and will always be a judgment call. Although all leaders agree this mandates some sort of disciplinary action, two schools of thought prevail:

- If the rep involved meets or exceeds quota on a regular basis and has no prior infractions, place them on probation for a period of time.
- Regardless of the amount of money involved, the rep lied. That action has serious ramifications including potentially damaging the company's reputation. Terminate their employment. No questions asked.

> Quick tip: Every company follows a different protocol for probation and termination. Before acting, consult with HR, the employee handbook, and an employment attorney for direction.

## Getting started

Reps occasionally discover a way to game the system, allowing them to falsify or manipulate information. Some stay quiet, not wanting anyone else to know about their behavior. Surprisingly, others "share the wealth" with a friend or two on staff.

Take the opportunity, no matter how unpleasant, disappointing, or unwelcome, to determine whether you have an isolated incident or a staff-wide problem. Spot check frequent contest winners and fully audit the last several sales contests. Take appropriate action once you know the extent of the problem.

## Prior bad acts

If this salesperson has demonstrated unethical behavior in the past, terminate their employment immediately. The other sales representatives already know or suspect this employee engages in dubious sales practices.

By keeping dishonest reps on staff, you both sanction their behavior and encourage the other sales representatives to cheat as well. Among those reps who would never consider cheating, this causes resentment and a loss of respect for the manager.

## Independent verification

Have a CSR (customer service representative) or another neutral party call the customer to verify the order in question. Simply have them say, "We're confirming a software order placed on July 30th for a delayed shipment of October 1st. Are our records correct?"

Managers sometimes resist this suggestion. They tell me, "The customer will immediately know what's up." Not necessarily, and you need not implicate the rep. Companies make mistakes and verify orders periodically. Reach out proactively, get the answer, and apologize for the error. One way or another, problems like this come to the surface. Fix it before the customer contacts the company.

## Create a plan

If company or sales leaders decide to give reps in this situation another chance, they need to be put on probation.

Formally document the infraction and outline the terms as follows:

| | |
|---|---|
| To: | Salesperson |
| cc: | President; Director of HR |
| From: | Sales Manager |
| Date: | August 10 |
| Re: | Sales Contest Violation |

---

On June 2, I announced a sales contest with the following rules:

Reps increasing their revenue from July of last year by 10 percent receive a gift certificate for $150. The rep increasing their July revenue by the highest percentage receives a gift certificate for $250.

Your individual goal was as follows:

| | |
|---|---|
| July (last year) | $63,000 |
| 10 percent increase | $6,300 |
| **Total** | **$69,300** |

Your sales for the period July 1st through July 31st totaled $71,500. You received the top prize of $250.

Contest rules stated that orders must be sold and installed by the last day of the month. Systems records show that on July 30th you entered a $2,800 order (#695477) for the Logan Corporation. On July 31st you put the order on hold. Then on August 1st you changed the installation date to October 1st. A company representative called the Logan Corporation to inquire about the order. The customer said they did not place that order.

The purpose of this memo is to inform you that we find you in violation of the rules of the contest. Consequently, I am obliged to issue this written warning. You are being placed on probation for the remainder of August, September, October, and November.

The terms are as follows:

- No participation in sales contests for the entirety of the probationary period
- Reimburse the company for the $250 gift certificate
- Be at or above 105 percent of quota at the end of the probationary period

Please be informed that any future or discoveries of past misconduct will result in immediate dismissal. It is my hope that you achieve these goals.

Manager _____

Employee _____

Date _____

[Note: This is a sample document. Please consult with appropriate parties for specific wording.]

The memo outlines the penalty for the rep's actions and gets placed in their employee file. Both the president and human resources know of the event. This being a judgment call, some will think it is adequate punishment, whereas others will feel it did not go far enough.

## Show the ROI

In pro-sales companies, sales leaders receive funding and support for sponsoring sales contests. Reps acting dishonestly are subject to disciplinary action of some kind. Although company leaders find it regrettable and disappointing, one salesperson's actions won't jeopardize future contests.

When sales leaders struggle to get bosses to fund or understand the importance of periodic sales contests, they worry about an infraction like this putting any future contests at risk. Prepare for that by showcasing any additional revenue brought in from previous contests.

| | Previous Revenue | Contest Total | Difference | % Difference | Contest Payouts |
|---|---|---|---|---|---|
| January Kick-off | $ 458,000 | $ 529,000 | $ 71,000 | 16% | $ 800 |
| March Madness | $ 537,000 | $ 562,000 | $ 25,000 | 5% | $ 350 |
| July Blast-off | $ 346,000 | $ 384,500 | $ 38,500 | 11% | $ 1,000 |
| Totals | $1,341,000 | $1,475,500 | $ 134,500 | 10% | $ 2,150 |

For $2,150, your sales team brought in an additional $134,500 in sales revenue: $2,150 / $134,500 = 1.5%. Most people would gladly accept that ROI.

## Present the plan to executives

Disappointing though this may be, don't try to handle it within the sales department. Direct supervisors, company presidents, and HR executives need to know. Tell them what happened. Share any documentation you've prepared during the discussion.

Once you've explained the situation, your boss will most likely ask for your opinion on the matter. Let him know how you personally feel the situation should be handled. After hearing you out and considering the various alternatives, he may agree with your suggestion or overrule you. Accept the decision with professionalism. Remember, this is a tough call.

## Future contests

Before the end of the meeting, discuss your plans to hold future sales contests. Remind all present of the importance of these events to reps facing the real problems such as a lack of motivation, rejection, and monotony. Let your boss know that cutting out any future contests based on the act of one rep punishes the salespeople that enjoy and get motivated by the challenge.

# Address the issue with the rep

In many cases, managers speak with reps about problems to gain an understanding of the situation (the inconsistent rep; the mediocre rep). With the unethical rep you deal not with a motivational or performance issue, but rather a rules, ethics, and potentially legal violation.

During a discussion involving unethical behavior of some type, I recommend having another person in the room with you and the rep (preferably from HR) for support and to ensure company protocol gets followed. Begin this conversation by reviewing the rules for the sales contest. See if they say anything. If they do not, present your findings. In my experience, reps react in four different ways:

- Ask questions ("Who told you this? Where did you get that information?")
- Deny ("I would never do anything like that. Your information is wrong.")
- Claim it was a misunderstanding
- Come clean ("It was a stupid thing to do. I'm so sorry.")

Typically, reps do this for three different reasons:

- Ego ("I can't let that other rep win the contest. I'm the better salesperson.")
- Thrill-seeking ("What if I could change that date and get away with it?")
- Desperation (unpaid bills or debt due to a personal or medical situation)

## Situation 1: Ask questions/denial/misunderstanding

If they ask questions, deny the charges, or suggest a misinterpretation, present the information again. If they continue to refute any culpability, make a simple statement like, "Unless you can present me with irrefutable evidence to the contrary, we'll move forward."

If they have no compelling argument, end the conversation. Have them wait in the meeting room while you discuss the situation with those involved. Then tell them whether you've decided to put them on probation or terminate their employment.

## Situation 2: Admission of guilt

If they admit wrongdoing immediately or after being re-shown the evidence, thank them for their candor. Then ask the following questions:

- Why did you do this?
- How did you do this?
- Are you aware of what you risked for $250?
- If I conduct research, will I come across another instance of cheating?
- If you were a manager, what would you do in my situation?
- What do you think the customer would advise me to do?
- In what way do you think this has impacted others in the organization?
- How do I know this won't happen again?
- Why shouldn't I fire you?

When answering the questions, do they seem embarrassed and sincerely sorry, or angry and hostile? Did they blame others or make excuses? Let their reaction help guide the decision-making.

As before, tell them you'll consider what they had to say. Have them wait in the meeting room, and then inform them of your decision.

## Follow-up conversation (with boss and other executives)

Review your discussion with the rep. Go over any new information coming to light during the conversation. Make the decision regarding the rep's future status with your organization.

## Follow-up conversation (with the rep)

Should you decide to terminate their employment, follow company protocol from that point forward.

When deciding to put reps on probation, present them with the document, confirm their understanding of the terms, and ask them to sign it right then.

If you hired the employee, I advise sales leaders to make a statement like:

"I hired you for a sales position in this organization. We're putting you on probation because, to our knowledge, you've been a model employee. By doing this, you've put our relationship with a good customer and potential future sales contests at risk. Professionally, I'm very disappointed in you."

If you inherited the employee, I recommend saying:

"When I was hired as sales manager, the president told me about the current sales staff. He had good things to say about you. We're putting you on probation…."

Allow them to say something if they so choose and then end the conversation.

## Reality check

Retaining an employee after a situation like this represents a real gamble. Though grateful not to be terminated, they will begin a job hunt.

Serial cheaters know you are on to them and they won't get away with anything going forward. For the sales rep making a "one-time" mistake, the pressure to perform combined with the damage to their reputation may prove to be too much.

Ramp up any ongoing recruitment efforts. You might be replacing this rep in the not too distant future.

> Quick tip: If you are asked to serve as a reference for this person in the future, let company policy determine how you handle the situation.

## Current staff

If your research shows this incident as a one-off on the part of one or two reps, no discussion needs to take place with the other salespeople. Disciplinary measures always remain confidential.

Should you find the problem to be staff-wide (rare, but it does happen), all parties would be subject to the same disciplinary action. Suspend all sales contests for a predetermined length of time.

## Hiring

Although this chapter talks about unethical behavior, it also deals with sales contests generally. Visit this subject during the interview process. Attitudes about sales contests reveal a lot about the motivation level of potential new hires. Ask questions like:

- Have you ever participated in a sales contest?
- Which one was your favorite?
- What did you win?
- If I created a contest just for you, what would it involve?

Most high-performing reps show tremendous enthusiasm for this subject, happily describing favorite contests and any prizes won.

## New hire orientation

Don't let a bad experience deter you from creating more sales contests. Used in the right way, at the right time, these competitions provide badly-needed motivation. Nowhere does this hold more truth than with a new hire.

Depending on the length of the sales cycle and the complexity of your product or service, it sometimes takes a while for even the most talented rep to close a sale. As early as possible, create a non-revenue based sales contest. Possibilities include reaching goals such as:

- Having 10 conversations with decision-makers.
- Conducting five product demonstrations.
- Sending out two proposals.

Having them participate in a sales contest tailored for new hires also provides sales leaders with the opportunity to talk about the company's policies on ethical behavior.

## Leadership opportunities

Forward-thinking sales executives advocate for their reps. They come up with good ideas that don't always go as planned. Sometimes, the very rep or reps they're fighting for undermine their efforts.

Even when reps disappoint, managers should remain undeterred, especially when they know a particular idea to be in the best interest of the company and sales staff. Great sales leaders acknowledge feeling let down while continuing to foster a motivated, thriving sales department.

## Summary checklist

### Unethical behavior review and checklist

- Clarify situation.
- Research:
  - Specifics of the order in question
  - Previous sales contest results
  - Other reps' orders from the same contest
  - Overall success of previous contests
- Present situation to executives.
- Speak with rep.
- Decide on probation or termination.

## Resolution

Tyler's eyes flashed with anger when Charles confronted him about the falsified order. He denied it with such vehemence that Charles nearly ended the conversation to go back and re-check the facts.

Instead, he took a deep breath and went through the information again. Mid-conversation, Tyler's tone changed. He became calmer, saying, "C'mon Charles, you know me. I wouldn't do something like that. I win these contests all the time."

He replied, "Tyler, wait here. I'll be back to let you know what we decide." Tyler said nothing in response.

When the president learned Tyler denied all charges, he told Charles and the HR director to terminate his employment. "Logan has been a valued client for years. We can't have a rep like Tyler working for our company."

Surprisingly, Tyler teared up when informed of the decision. Charles stood up, shook Tyler's hand, and said, "This was absolutely unnecessary. Grow and learn from it. Good luck to you."

He thought about Tyler and the whole sorry mess for many weeks afterward.

# Chapter 9
# **Misaligned Territories**

Interviewing at Papaya Storm, sales manager Gabe learned about the oddly configured sales territories. For the chance to work at Papaya Storm, the hottest cloud software company on the market, he'd find a way to deal with the problem.

Marcus, company founder and president, had always managed the sales staff. He partnered with resellers in some parts of the country, but wanted a dedicated sales force calling on customers in territories close to headquarters.

The team superstar, Eric, covered Metro West, Monday through Thursday. He asked for an area far north of the city as well—near his lake house. He could drive up Friday morning, call on his accounts, and arrive at his second home that evening.

Eric being his only salesperson at the time, Marcus agreed to it. Why not? Eric could have his pick of employers. In the years since, he proved to be a great hire, always making a full day of Fridays, and never using his lake house as an excuse to quit early.

Marcus then hired Natalie. Semi-retired, she wanted to cover a small number of accounts downtown. After they agreed to a more modest pay-check and quota, that arrangement was successful as well.

Somehow he convinced Sarah, a young, aggressive salesperson, to agree to fit her territory in and around Eric's and Natalie's.

Marcus expected Gabe to hire two new salespeople shortly after he started. Gabe called Diane, a former colleague, to tell her about the job. He thought her skill set would be a great match for Papaya Storm.

During their first interview, she asked about her territory. As he explained, she looked at him quizzically. Later, she called him and said, "Gabe, I'm flattered you called me. I'd enjoy working with you again, but not at Papaya Storm. That sales territory is all over the place. I just don't get a good feeling about it."

Marcus hired Gabe to lead the sales force and hit aggressive growth goals. The odd territories might prevent him from hiring enough reps to do that. Ultimately, it could cost him his job. He has to address this issue.

---

### Problem summary

Current sales reps

- Asked for specific geographic territories
- Had sound reasons for the requests
- Established relationships with decision-makers in the areas
- Have strong sales skills

Sales manager

- Wanted to work for a hot software company
- Inherited solid sales staff
- Given aggressive revenue numbers to hit
- Must hire additional sales reps
- Finds hiring difficult with odd territory configurations

Enthusiastic about a company's product or service, sales managers happily accept an offer of employment. Then reality hits. A seemingly acceptable problem looms large and must be fixed.

Founders bring companies to a certain point. Their sales-related decisions represented sound choices *at the time*. The current sales set-up likely grew out of a lack of capital and/or sales management expertise.

Most company leaders need dedicated sales management help after a certain point in the evolution of the business. That manager must jump in and correct any missteps.

---

Quick tip: This situation could also apply to conflicts between a field and inside sales group or geographic and national accounts.

---

## Sales territories

Protected territories (geographic or vertical) enable sales reps to familiarize themselves with and intensively work a particular area or market segment. Salespeople get assigned certain zip codes, counties, multi-state areas, or specific industries. Longtime customers provide referrals to other companies. Some reps join local business groups.

Meandering territories upset this balance. A coaching client of mine who was facing this problem once told me he was "sick of seeing his salespeople wave to each other as they visited customers in the same area."

## Getting started

Before suggesting any changes, objectively summarize the situation in each territory by analyzing the performance for three years running (where possible).

### Eric / Territory A (Metro West and Metro North)

The $1.4-million-dollar and 108-percent increase during a three-year period speak for themselves. He does an excellent job with Metro West.

| | Year 1 | Year 2 | Year 3 | Difference Yr 1/Yr 3 | % Difference |
|---|---|---|---|---|---|
| Metro West | 1,300,000 | $1,860,000 | 2,700,000 | $1,400,000 | 108% |
| | Year 1 | Year 2 | Year 3 | Difference Yr 1/Yr 3 | % Difference |
| Metro North | $ 620,000 | $657,000 | $683,000 | $63,000 | 10% |

However, the Metro North territory speaks for itself as well. He covers it, but that's about all. The long drive prevents him from spending a lot of time in this area. He's opened no new accounts.

More importantly, the territory has changed. Even five years ago, few companies had headquarters that far north. With several new office parks being built and corporations relocating to the area, the revenue potential has grown considerably.

### Natalie / Territory B (Downtown)

The 11-percent increase realized during a three-year period results more from price increases than a real effort on the part of the downtown rep.

| Year 1 | Year 2 | Year 3 | Difference Yr 1/Yr 3 | % Difference |
|---|---|---|---|---|
| $440,000 | $481,000 | $489,000 | $49,000 | 11% |

Although she excels at maintaining her current customer base, no growth takes place. Natalie does no prospecting and opens no new accounts. With a hot software app, she should be doubling business.

### Sarah / Territory C (Hodgepodge)

This rep covers a small part of downtown as well as areas northeast and south of the city.

| | Year 1 | Year 2 | Year 3 | Difference Yr 1/Yr 3 | % Diff-erence |
|---|---|---|---|---|---|
| **Metro South** | $650,000 | $768,000 | $884,000 | $234,000 | 36% |
| | **Year 1** | **Year 2** | **Year 3** | **Difference Yr 1/Yr 3** | **% Diff-erence** |
| **Downtown (partial)** | $295,000 | $314,000 | $325,000 | $30,000 | 10% |
| | **Year 1** | **Year 2** | **Year 3** | **Difference Yr 1/Yr 3** | **% Diff-erence** |
| **Northeast** | $370,000 | $392,000 | $410,000 | $40,000 | 11% |

Sarah realizes solid growth in Metro South, spends little time downtown, and focuses only on the largest accounts in her northeast territory.

## Summary

The three reps bring in a total of more than $5.4 million dollars: Eric ($3,383,000), Natalie ($497,000), and Sarah ($1,619,000).

- Eric cannot adequately cover the northern part of his territory.
- Natalie focuses only on select accounts.
- Sarah works only certain sections of her geographic area.

## Create a plan

For the time being, forget past promises, personalities, and tenure. Rearranging territories calls for objectivity. Sales managers in this situation benefit from using territory mapping software that knows neither favoritism nor seniority while striving to balance market opportunity and workload.

After entering the data, view the software's suggested territories for business potential, territory coverage, and geographical boundaries.

> Quick tip: Some territory mapping software programs integrate with a company's CRM system.

## Be a positive change agent

This manager supervises talented salespeople, representing the company well when they call on valued clients. The problem involves the companies *not* getting called on and the amount of travel time between the clients. It is about lost opportunity.

When confronting imbalanced territories, avoid being seen as the manager taking accounts away. Advocate for new business and company growth.

Demonstrate the potential additional revenue with balanced and covered territories:

| Rep | Adjusted Territories | Projected Revenue |
| --- | --- | --- |
| Eric | Metro West (Expanded) | $ 3,900,000 |
| New Hire | Metro North (Expanded) | $ 1,400,000 |
| Natalie | Downtown (Expanded) | $ 2,650,000 |
| Sarah | Metro South | $ 1,300,000 |
| New Hire | Northeast | $ 850,000 |
| **Total** | | **$ 10,100,000** |

The territories in total, as they exist today, produce $5,499,000 in revenue. Properly aligned, the company realizes $10 million in revenue, an increase of 119 percent or $4.6 million dollars.

# Present the plan to executives

Company owners, presidents, and CEOs know a territory problem exists. They might lack the know-how or time to resolve the issue. Others look to avoid the confrontation a change like this involves.

Without saying so in the interview, they *want* and *expect* the new sales leaders to take care of the issue. Fair? No. Reality? Yes.

Consider their fears, prior to broaching the subject:

- Disgruntled reps quitting and going to work for a competitor
- Long-time clients expressing displeasure with change
- Loss of sales revenue that sometimes accompanies territory realignments

Begin the discussion by reviewing the charts, graphs, and maps you've put together. Segue to the problems involved in staying with the status quo including:

- Low percentage of new business.
- Rep complaints about lack of fairness and territory potential.
- Reps managing, not working territories.
- Stagnant company growth.
- Industry reputation.
- Hiring difficulties.

Discuss the pros and cons of different plans. Consider what your boss has to say. Together, make decisions leading to appropriate territory alignment.

## Protect company assets

The work involved in a project like this, coupled with anxiety about dealing with the reps, leads you to sometimes forget about the most important party—the customer. Before speaking with the reps, decide how these territory changes get communicated to your valued clients.

Look at the list of accounts. Together, decide which clients:

- Require an in-person visit.
- Could be told by conference call or Skype.
- Are small enough for an e-mail or phone call.

Once you've reached agreement, share this plan at a sales staff meeting.

## Address the issue with the rep

With most sales-related problems (reps not prospecting or CRM non-compliance) company leaders do nothing to cause these difficulties. You need their *support* and *approval* to act on and solve issues through sales department policies and disciplinary action. After that, as sales leader, you handle the difficulty.

With the issue of oddly configured territories, the company leader created the problem. It pre-dated the sales manager's employment there by many years. I recommend conversations with the reps (individually and as a group) about the territory changes be held with both the president and sales leader present.

Keep all conversations confidential (and ask them to do so also) until you've agreed to a plan for each salesperson.

## The rep's perspective

Using mapping software, reviewing the numbers and creating spreadsheets helps you prove a case for realigning the territories. None of it prepares you for the actual conversations with the salespeople.

Reps carefully guard the original custom territory arrangements struck with a company founder. Few welcome any change. Call these territory deals by the right name—a perk or benefit like any other. An emotional attachment exists.

Managers dealing with misaligned territories have to:

- Expand or shrink territories.
- Reassign accounts.
- Change job descriptions.

Think about each salesperson individually. Consider:

- What they were promised.
- What they're giving up.
- How this decision affects them.
- Potential for leaving the company.
- Concerns about income loss.

In my experience, reps react in three ways:

- Whine about how unfair this is, given the investment of time they've put in.
- Get angry, then threaten to quit and go to the competition.
- Become territorial, claiming only they can work with certain accounts.

Come up with a list of likely objections and prepare to address each one.

# Example 1: Eric (Metro West and North)

Manager: "As a company, we're making some changes, one of which involves you. I know your current territory works really well for you and your family. You've increased business in Metro West by 108 percent during the last three years and we value that contribution.

"That territory made sense when the company was in startup mode. With a plan to grow at least 25 percent next year, we need to make adjustments to everyone's territories. We'd like you to focus on an expanded Metro West. I'll be hiring a rep to work the northern area you've been covering."

Rep: "I took this job with the understanding that I could spend Fridays working in the area near my second home. If you take that away, I'll accept a position with iRoute. Their internal recruiter calls me about once a month."

Statements like this put managers on the defensive. They think, "Oh no. They have another offer. I better back down."

The iRoute recruiter probably *does* call the rep. That company *might* be interested in speaking with him. But guess what, that recruiter calls many candidates.

I've dealt with the problem of a talented rep threatening to quit and go elsewhere many, many times. Stay calm. In a measured voice, ask simple, direct questions including:

- How long have you been speaking with iRoute?
- What would the opportunity at iRoute look like?
- Would they offer you Metro West and the northern part of the state?

- What would your first-year earning potential be?
- How serious are you about going to work for them?

Phrase any other inquiries in a businesslike way. This approach alters the conversation. The more you inquire about the specifics of the offer (if indeed one exists) from another company, the more uncomfortable the rep becomes. Most change the subject and focus on the matter at hand.

## Example 2

Manager: "As a company, we're making some changes…[continues with the same statement as in Example 1]."

Rep: "Make any changes necessary—in other territories. Don't touch mine. How many salespeople are out there that can close deals like I can?"

Manager: "That might be so. Let's look at the numbers and discuss some interesting possibilities."

Rep: "Judy Samuelson at Bolton won't work with anyone but me. She's said so many times. You take me out of that account, you'll lose her business altogether. Make the territory changes elsewhere."

Managers working at companies of all sizes and different industries get confronted with this statement. In a straightforward and calm manner remind the rep that Bolton is the *company's customer*, not the rep's, and that Judy Samuelson is an employee, not an owner, at Bolton.

Yes, companies enjoy the continuity of being called on by the same rep. Few expect the same rep to handle their account permanently, knowing resignations and reassignments occur. Though the rep might not suspect it, some welcome a change in personnel.

When or if reorganizations take place, customers worry about one thing only: being well taken care of. When all parties concerned (president, sales manager, and customer service) assure the account they'll be on top of things, most accounts accept the transition. Sometimes clients are even happier, as a new rep brings a fresh perspective.

## Moving the conversation along

Listen to the rep's objections, giving them your full and serious attention. Address those that you can, get back to them on others. At a certain point say, "I understand your concerns about these changes. We'll meet again and address them specifically. For now, let's look at what I've prepared."

Instead of getting upset or dictatorial, pique the rep's interest. They'll be curious about what you have to say. Go over the spreadsheets. Review the numbers. To make an impression and underscore the necessity of territory realignment, use visuals.

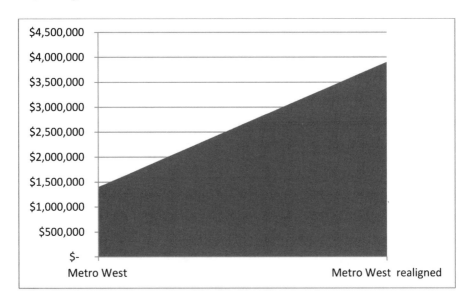

Eric sold $2,700,000 in software in the smaller Metro West territory. By working an expanded territory closer to home, he can see the substantial projected increase ($3,900,000).

Next to the founder, the role of salesperson represents the most entrepreneurial job in the organization. Business savvy salespeople regard their territories as their own micro-companies. Between the lost revenue and lack of consistent territory coverage, the need for change becomes more evident to them.

## Negotiations with reps

From Eric's point of view, the realignment forces him to:

- Give up a personally attractive territory configuration.
- Terminate strong relationships with companies and buyers.

- Cold call in the expanded Metro West Territory.
- Question the impact of this on his income.

With his talents, he represents a genuine flight risk. Consider offering commission to both he and his replacement, on sales to his old accounts, for a period of one year (or another appropriate length of time). Include his working with, advising, and making introductions for the new rep as part of the deal.

Sign him up for training or coaching for cold calling. It might have been quite some time since he's had to open new accounts. Really think about the rep and making this transition more appealing. Gestures like this go a long, long way.

Many leaders balk at having to do any of this. I advise them to compare the total costs of replacing a rep of that caliber versus paying double commission for a period of time. Most see the wisdom of the plan.

Rep by rep, consider what they might be losing or gaining in terms of their territory. In advance, determine who you might have to incent to stay. Think it through.

## Accountability

Prior to the reorganization, reps at this company treated parts of their territories casually. They took care of the largest accounts and saw other clients when they could. During individual conversations, be clear this behavior changes going forward.

Let reps know they need to use territory planning software to determine optimum coverage. No more ignoring certain accounts or areas due to lack of time or too many miles. Accounts must be called on at intervals appropriate to their total revenue contribution. Inform the reps that territory coverage will be discussed during performance reviews.

## Current staff

Once you and your boss have met with each rep and reached agreement on the new territories, it's time to address the entire sales group.

Ask the president to make the opening remarks. Have him talk about the reasons for and necessity of the realignment including: aggressive growth goals, territory coverage, and new business acquisition. Be sure he encourages questions.

Share the new territory map with the group. Talk about realignments allowing the company to expand the sales force. Ask the reps if they know of any salespeople at other companies who might be interested in speaking with you about the open positions.

Don't discuss any underperformance problems or lack of account coverage at this meeting. You've gone over that in the one-on-ones. Keep the meeting positive and forward-focused.

# Hiring

Many hours have gone into this realignment project. Remember that when speaking to and negotiating with future applicants. Don't create another difficult situation for yourself.

Be clear about available open territories and the customers within each one. Get involved in a territory negotiation only if it benefits your *company*. Generally, avoid protracted negotiations with a candidate who has yet to bring in any revenue at all for your company.

Occasionally, candidates ask about continuing to call on a particular client not in their new territory. Your own rep might be willing to trade that client for another in the new rep's territory. Though rare, I've seen this happen. Where you see a win/win for all concerned, consider it.

Lastly, include questions about territory coverage during the interviews:

- How did they determine optimum territory coverage in previous positions?
- Did they have a formalized plan?

Understand their overall approach to this critical component of a sales position.

# New hire orientation

Offer new hires training on the call planning software and make territory coverage part of the discussion early on. Be certain they understand the value of each account and how often they should be called on. Hold them accountable to scheduled visits.

## Leadership opportunities

Sometimes sales leaders grapple with challenges involving only one or two reps. In other cases, a problem affects the *entire* sales force. When this happens, to move a company forward, the previous way of running sales must change.

Solving the problem involves compromise, re-structuring, budget appropriation, and sometimes parting company with some salespeople. Basically, it calls into play a different kind of leadership including: risk taking, handling confrontation, resolve, and the discipline to see the changes through.

Sales leaders able to handle sales force-wide adjustments gain the respect of bosses, peers, and the sales staff.

## Summary checklist

## Misaligned territories review and checklist

- Clarify problem.
- Run territory productivity reports.
- Reconfigure territories for:
  - Revenue growth
  - Appropriate coverage
  - Future hiring ability
- Present potential solutions to direct supervisor.
- Meet one-on-one with each salesperson.
  - Discuss new territories
  - Negotiate where necessary
- Address current staff.
- Hold reps accountable for appropriate territory coverage.

## Resolution

When Marcus and Gabe told Eric he'd have to give up the northern part of his territory, he wasn't too pleased. For the next week Eric was distant and out of the office a lot. His CRM entries were sparse. Marcus and Gabe suspected he was job hunting.

After that week, he seemed like his old self. He asked to be paid full commission for one year on any sales from the accounts in the northern part of his former territory. They compromised on full commission for six months and 50 percent for the next six. Eric agreed to make introductions for and mentor whoever takes over the territory.

Though he thinks it's a long shot that any company would offer him the ideal territory he enjoyed for years at Papaya Storm, Gabe still worries about Eric resigning.

Natalie neither wanted to work full-time nor cover an expanded territory. At his previous company, Gabe managed an inside sales group calling on accounts below a certain dollar volume. After he reorganized and hired for the new territories, he wanted to form an inside sales group at Papaya Storm. Why not start with Natalie? He offered her a three-day work week, contacting lower revenue customers by phone. Reluctantly, she agreed to give it a try.

Of all people, Sarah surprised him. Thinking she'd jump at the chance to cover all of downtown, she seemed hesitant. She told Gabe about her concerns taking over accounts Natalie had called on for years and, in a few cases, decades. They came up with a plan to make the first in-person call to Natalie's former customers together. Sarah seemed relieved.

A month later, during a quiet moment, Gabe called his former colleague Diane to see if she would reconsider his earlier offer. "Let's meet for lunch soon," he said, "we've made a few changes I'd like to discuss with you."

# Chapter 10
# The Selling Sales Manager

Company president John manages sales. Never having sold himself, he knows he does a poor job. He welcomes the other responsibilities that distract him from sales management obligations.

With only four salespeople, he doesn't feel justified in hiring a full-time sales manager. Instead, he offered Alisa, a high-performing rep, a selling sales management position. She had often expressed interest in managing salespeople one day.

John changed her comp plan, reduced her client load, and distributed her accounts among the other reps. Alisa agreed to work with her own accounts in the morning and in the late afternoon. From about 10 a.m. to 3 p.m., she would spend time with the salespeople.

Two reps, Guy and Rebecca, were excited about Alisa taking on management duties. They liked her and respected her sales ability. Vince was another story. Though he had never expressed any interest in management, he resented the position being given to Alisa. "Why her?" he asked John, right after the promotion was announced.

Day one on the job, Alisa walked into her office, ready to make prospecting calls before "wearing her management hat" at 10 a.m. But Rebecca was already in her office. She asked Alisa if she had a few minutes. Forty-five minutes later, they were still discussing her client issue.

The schedule she and John worked out quickly fell apart. As an "almost manager," she attended three times the meetings she had as a rep. When the CRM system went down, she spent hours with IT. After years of using the same proposal template, marketing insisted it needed to be revised and updated immediately.

Rebecca constantly needed guidance on every sales issue. Vince acted standoffish, rolling his eyes at suggestions she made. Only Guy appeared comfortable with the new arrangement, respecting Alisa's schedule and asking when she had time available.

A month into the job, John called Alisa into his office. "Louis at Tribeqq called me today. He claimed getting his calls returned has become an issue. Any truth to that?"

Yes, Alisa thought to herself. And soon you'll be hearing from other clients. Everything was falling apart.

---

### Problem summary

Selling sales manager

- Communicated interest in management position
- Accepted hybrid position
- Agreed to schedule and job responsibilities
- Feels ineffective with reps, coworkers, and customers

Sales reps

- One reacted badly to the promotion of a peer
- Another demands constant attention

Marketing
- Has expectations of sales leader

Company president
- Disliked managing the sales team
- Tried to create a reasonable schedule and expectations
- Sees selling manager's client relationships deteriorate
- Deals with complaints from reps and other managers

A "selling manager" position allows a rep interested in managing a sales team to learn the job while continuing to contribute on the revenue side. For a small division within a larger organization or a smaller company with few reps, the dual role represents an economical option.

However, the selling sales manager position usually veers rapidly out of control. Why? *Because it rarely works.* Regardless of company size, managers should manage. Reps should sell. The two jobs require completely different skill sets, talents, and motivators.

Unless absolutely necessary, I advise companies not to take this path. If they insist, I recommend following the advice provided throughout thischapter. Before taking the leap, be realistic about the high likelihood of failure.

## Getting started

Prior to speaking with any rep about the position, consider the differences between salespeople and sales managers:

| Sales Representative | Sales Manager |
|---|---|
| Works for the customer | Works for the company |
| Individual contributor | Accomplishes goals through others |
| Tasked with individual revenue goal | Tasked with group revenue goal |
| Calls on customers regularly | Accompanies sales rep on customer visits |
| Advocates for customer | Upholds company policies and procedures |
| Gets along reasonably well with peers | Has hire/fire power over reps |
| Uses resources to make themselves successful | Provides resources to make reps successful |

I ask company leaders contemplating the selling/management role to picture someone continuously changing hats or moving from one side of the desk to the other—all day long. When they do, the duality of the job becomes clearer.

# Create a plan

Presidents hiring for this position often skip the interview process, opting instead to select the rep on the current staff they feel would fit the best.

Reps being considered for this new role have already proven themselves as salespeople and employees. For now, disregard reps' past sales accomplishments. View them as management candidates and proceed accordingly.

Think of this role as one tricky high-wire act. The more effort you put into the pre-planning of the position, the more you increase the chances of success.

# Write a job description

Take the time to create a formal job description. Consider the responsibilities of this new position. Collaborate on the document with human resources and/or a few trusted advisers for their comments.

---

**Selling sales manager duties include:**

**Sales revenue**

- Achieve and exceed sales revenue goal through the sales team
- Work with president to set individual and team goals
- Prepare sales forecasts by product and territory
- Track sales team metrics and report data to president on a regular basis
- Collaborate with department leaders on sales-related initiatives

**Sales team development**

- Develop direct reports through coaching, motivating, and improving sales skills and product knowledge
- Work with and observe the sales representatives on a regular basis
- Create sales contests to motivate sales reps
- Organize the recruitment effort for new salespeople
- Implement an appraisal system to monitor performance

**Company values**

- Ensure customer satisfaction
- Uphold company vision, values, and policies
- Act as a fair arbiter amongst salespeople on issues of conflict

**Sales duties include:**

**Territory**

- Achieve sales revenue goal
- Cover geographic territory/assigned accounts

---

- Follow call plan generated by territory planning software
- Resolve customer complaints and problems
- Generate proposals

**CRM**

- Input sales data and notes in CRM system
- Submit required sales reports on due dates

**Meetings**

- Work company sponsored booth at assigned trade shows and conventions
- Maintain professional and technical knowledge

## Develop a compensation plan

Salespeople usually receive a base salary and commission or bonus (or both) based on their sales production. The more they sell, the greater their earnings. Sales managers typically earn a base salary and commission or bonus (or both) on the total revenue produced by the group they supervise. The more the group sells, the greater the sales manager's earnings.

With the selling sales manager still carrying an individual quota, I recommend a two-part commission plan. One part incents them for increasing sales in their reduced territory, whereas the second part incents them to motivate each rep to exceed their individual quota.

Alisa's compensation plan as a sales rep was as follows:

| **Sales representative compensation plan** | | |
|---|---|---|
| Base salary: | $52,500 | |
| Target Performance: | Annual: $1,345,000 | Quarterly: $336,250 |
| Commission: | $0–$336,250: | 3% |
| | $336,251 ~: | 5% |

Her boss John reduced her sales quota to $689,000 annually/$172,250 quarterly. He divided up her remaining accounts, worth $656,000, among the remaining three reps:

|  | Quota | Additional Revenue | New Quota |
|---|---|---|---|
| Guy | $ 1,350,000 | $ 300,000 | $ 1,650,000 |
| Vince | $ 1,295,000 | $ 250,000 | $ 1,545,000 |
| Rebecca | $ 1,310,000 | $ 106,000 | $ 1,416,000 |
| Totals | $ 3,955,000 | $ 656,000 | $ 4,611,000 |

For her compensation plan as selling sales manager, John increases her base salary, keeps the commission for her individual sales the same, and adds a commission structure based on the group's overall performance:

### Selling sales manager compensation plan

Base salary:          $65,000

Individual
Target Performance:  Annual: $689,000     Quarterly: $172,250

Group
Target Performance:  Annual: $4,611,000   Quarterly: $1,152,750

**Individual Quarterly Commission**  **Group Quarterly Commission**

$0–$172,250:  3%                 $0–$1,152,750:  .005%

$172,251 ~:  5%                  $1,152,751 ~:  .007%

**Quarterly Earnings Example**

**Quarterly Sales**

Individual Quarterly Sales:   $197,000

Group Quarterly Sales:        $1,193,000

| Earnings | | |
|---|---|---|
| Base salary (3 months): | | $16,250 |
| Individual Commission: | $172,250 @ 3% | $5,168 |
| | $24,750 @ 5% | $1,238 |
| Group Commission | $1,152,750 @ .005% | $5,763 |
| | $40,250 @ .007% | $282 |
| **Total** | | **$28,701** |
| **Annualized Estimate** (4 quarters) | | **$114,804** |

Use the compensation plan that works best for your organization. Numbers and percentages used in the plan above are only suggestions. Comp plans differ by industry and geographic area.

## Evaluate for competency

Make no assumptions about a talented rep's ability to manage. Avoid basing your decision on emotion or a rep's prior *sales* accomplishments.

Ask salespeople in consideration for the job to take a sales management assessment. If the test scores indicate a lack skills needed for the job, don't move forward. They aren't right for the position and it won't work out.

Reps failing as selling sales managers find themselves in a tough spot. Pride might prevent them from returning to the sales staff. Regrettably, they often seek employment elsewhere. You've now lost one of your better reps.

## Interview

Speak with peers and do some online research. Consider engaging the services of an expert. Do what's necessary to learn how to conduct an interview for this position. Sales managers accomplish goals *through* others. To gauge the candidate's ability to do so, ask questions such as:

- How would you go about getting the best performance from a salesperson?
- Have you ever created a plan for someone else and then put it into place? How did it work out?

- What is your experience mentoring and developing another individual? How did you approach that task?
- If a salesperson made a mistake with a valued customer, what course of action would you take to rectify that situation?
- What would you do during your first few weeks as the selling manager?

As you would with an outside applicant, hold more than one interview with the candidate. Gain a solid understanding of how they view and would structure the job.

## Outline the parameters

Thinking that having fewer accounts gives the selling sales manager more time to work with the reps, executives decrease the size of their sales territory. It sounds simple. Unfortunately, it isn't.

Selling sales managers might push hard to maintain their existing territory. Don't give in. To ensure their success in this role, assign the selling sales manager a limited number of carefully edited accounts. Set reasonable quotas, especially during that first year.

Be realistic about lead follow-up and prospecting. They lack the time for open-ended activities like these. It just won't happen.

## Train

Let's suppose that everything points toward your candidate succeeding in this position. An assessment shows they have the right skills with perhaps a few identified gaps. The interview process goes well. The rep seems to have a reasonable grasp of what the job entails.

Further increase the chances for success. Sign them up for a sales management training course. Not a management course, a *sales* management course. Have them attend the training (or at least start it) before their first day on the job. This gives them the opportunity to:

- Work with and learn from experienced instructors.
- Chat with and trade experiences with peers in the same position.
- Develop a professional network of fellow sales executives.

You are asking them to juggle two vastly different roles—one where they have experience and one where they have none. The instruction gives them an added measure of confidence.

---

Quick tip: After the initial training period, selling sales managers gravitate more toward managing or selling. If they lean decidedly more toward sales and away from the management, discuss the situation with them. If after a reasonable period of time nothing changes, put them back in sales.

To avoid having them leave the company, give them a slightly different or elevated sales role, like major accounts, if possible.

---

## Limit initiatives

As company leader, you got to sales management tasks when you could, so a lot of sales-related initiatives went unaddressed. Logically, you'd assign the new selling sales manager responsibility for these projects now.

Not just yet. During the first year, keep a tight rein on the number of additional projects you ask them to take on such as:

- Researching and selecting a new CRM system.
- Updating the sales performance review.
- Instituting a new lead gen tracking system.

If you want the selling manager to succeed, act as their gatekeeper. Stop other departments from trying to dominate their time by providing some air cover. Keep them focused on their top priorities: selling and managing the reps.

For these and other projects, work with the selling sales manager to set priorities and stick with them.

---

Quick tip: Select a target end date for this job. If they succeed in the position, phase them in as a full-time manager as soon as possible. No one lasts forever in a hybrid position like this. The selling sales manager eventually gets burned out and starts to job hunt for a dedicated sales management position.

---

Don't wait and hope for the best. This won't change. Those really interested in management look for opportunities to give away more and more of their sales responsibilities. They want to supervise the reps on a full-time basis.

## Act as backup

You have a vested interest in the success of this new position. For the first year, act as the backup manager when salespeople need assistance. If you've worked out a Tuesday/Friday selling schedule for the selling sales manager, keep your own calendar light for those two days.

Make yourself reasonably available to the reps. When a rep takes advantage of your time (and the average performers will), don't let them get away with it. Let them know you feel they could have handled the situation on their own. Call them out on it if they start to turn everything into an emergency to get attention. Manage the situation.

## The best gift

New managers need ways to assert their authority in a positive way. To help this process, I advise company leaders to have each salesperson to take a sales assessment. Go over the results with the new selling manager. Have them review the results with the reps.

When the selling manager was a rep and you had the entire sales staff take an assessment, you would never have shared the other rep's results with her. The information was confidential.

Now she manages these reps. Though she worked with them previously and has some familiarity with their work style, she benefits tremendously from the unbiased information contained in the assessments.

As new managers review the results with reps, they establish themselves as the boss. They now have data the reps don't necessarily want them to have (information on their weaknesses). This changes their former peer-to-peer relationship.

The assessments saves most managers hours of time spent observing and trying to understanding the pros and cons of the reps' approach to sales. The impartial facts allow them to interact with and provide coaching insights immediately.

Spend the money necessary to assess the reps. Hand the results to your new selling manager. It's the best investment you'll make all year.

## Present the plan to executives

Once you've finalized the details, seek out a second opinion or a review of the plan. Talk to trusted networking colleagues. If you belong to one, get feedback from peers in a roundtable-type group. Some may have dealt with this situation before. They might offer valuable suggestions.

Then present the plan to anyone you report to such as a CEO, chairman, or board of directors.

## Address the issue with the rep

When they've accepted the position, take another look at the specifics of the job together. Adjust some of the particulars if necessary. Most new managers have been thinking about the job for some time. They have a few ideas of their own.

## Account list

Review and refine the rep's new, smaller account list. Ask for their thoughts on the various customers' revenue potential.

Don't let them heroically agree to call on more accounts than they can reasonably manage. It's better to give them fewer and add on later than to give them too many. They have no idea what they're getting themselves into.

## Agree to a schedule

I've seen every imaginable combination of schedule for a selling manager: sales rep from 8:00 a.m. to noon, then sales manager from 1:00 p.m. to 5:30 p.m.; sales rep on Tuesday and Thursday to selling manager on Monday, Wednesday, and Friday; or no schedule at all.

No matter the type of sales group (inside, field, remote), the only way I know to make this work involves the selling manager being *totally unavailable* as a sales manager for a minimum of two days a week.

If they manage field reps at a central office, they should stay in the field themselves several days a week. They go nowhere near the office. Those who supervise an inside group should make their calls from an office down the hall, on another floor, or from their home. When all of the reps work remotely, the selling manager stays unavailable by text, e-mail, Skype, or any other form of communication.

If they check their cell phone messages right after a sales call, they will respond. It's human nature. Then they get dragged into managing on the run. Suddenly, they're late, distracted, or unprepared for the next call. The clients see this and don't like it. The dual position begins to unravel.

Yes, sometimes emergencies occur. Have the reps go through you on the days your selling manager is indisposed. You make the call about the situation being an emergency or not. For a really urgent situation, the selling manager should get back to you. If this happens all the time, you have a problem.

Company leaders struggle with this concept. In their mind, sales managers remain available at all times to work with the reps. And they're right: A sales manager should be. But they manage a *selling* sales manager.

Salespeople need to get into a rhythm to succeed in sales. Making one sales call, dealing with reps, and then trying to make a few prospecting calls doesn't work out. For now, you need your former rep to sell and manage.

Together, select the days of the week you think would work best for your selling sales manager and the reps. See how it goes. Experiment with different days until you both agree you've hit on the best combination possible. Get input from the sales staff.

No ideal schedule exists for this job. All parties involved must get comfortable with an imperfect situation.

## Month/quarter end

Financially it doesn't make sense for you to carry a full-time sales manager on payroll at this point, so your selling sales manager still carries a quota. Be sure and honor that.

If need be, during the final days of the month and last week or so of the quarter, allow them to spend the majority of time closing their own deals. Ask which reps need help putting the final touches on a proposal or could benefit from management presence on a joint sales call. Then do your part.

# Meetings

During the first quarter, make room in your schedule for at least two one-on-one meetings per week with the new selling manager. Select the dates for the bi-weekly get-togethers at the beginning of each month. Put together an agenda. No other work should take precedence.

Use this time to advise and counsel. You've managed people for years. Share your experiences. Encourage selling managers to speak openly about their experiences in the new position. Discuss areas of difficulty and conflict. Provide support.

On the selling manager's side, they need to meet with each rep one-on-one on a weekly basis. Quick phone calls to chat about a customer and reviewing CRM notes don't count. They should hold old-school weekly meetings with agendas. This establishes them as the sales leader and cuts down on the impromptu demands on their time.

## Current staff

Just because all or most of the reps enjoyed working on the same sales team with the new selling manager doesn't mean they'll like reporting to her. Don't be caught off guard by jealousy, rebellion, or over-dependency on the part of any of the reps. Get out in front of it.

Speak with each one individually. Explain your reasons for creating the new position and choosing this particular person. Talk about what you see as the benefits of having someone in this new role.

If a rep wonders why you didn't select them, be candid. Let them know what they should work on if they want to be considered for the position in the future. If they don't like the new selling sales manager or feel she lacks the right qualifications, listen respectfully. Resist arguing. Instead, ask questions. Reiterate your reasons for choosing the rep.

At the end of the conversation, make sure they understand the decision has been made. Going forward, they report directly to the new selling sales manager. As an employee of the organization, you expect them to work together with their new supervisor.

## The mediocre salesperson

In all sizes of companies and across all industries, this individual takes up most of your selling sales manager's time—the average performer. Those reps just making or just missing their goal demand the most management attention.

| | Quota | Sales | Difference | % Difference |
|---|---|---|---|---|
| **Guy** | $ 1,350,000 | $ 1,580,000 | $ 230,000 | 117% |
| **Vince** | $ 1,295,000 | $ 1,478,000 | $ 183,000 | 114% |
| **Rebecca** | $ 1,310,000 | $ 1,324,000 | $ 14,000 | 101% |

Identify the mediocre reps and deal with them proactively, not reactively. In the first meeting, don't let on that you think they'll ask for the most attention. Instead, ask about their expectations for this newly created position. Find out how they would deal with a difficult customer problem if the selling manager wasn't available.

Discuss the selling manager's schedule. Explain the need for them to spend several days a week focused on sales. They won't stop clamoring for attention. But it allows you to refer back to this conversation and keep them in check.

## Announcing the promotion

Once you've met with all the necessary parties and spoken with them about the new position, send an e-mail notifying the entire organization. This gesture gives additional credibility to your new selling sales manager.

Next, formally announce it at a sales staff meeting. Include managers who interact with the selling sales manager frequently. Have lunch brought in. Make it a festive occasion.

Say a few words about the history of the company and then share your thinking on the need for a selling sales manager. Tell the group how you see the position as being beneficial to everyone. Ask the new selling sales manager to make a few remarks. Everyone appreciates this kind of effort.

# Hiring

Most applicants view working for a company with a dedicated sales manager as a plus. Sales managers offer coaching, mentoring, and guidance.

This new position represents a step forward for your company. Talk about it in a positive light. Explain how it works and answer any questions candidates have.

## New hire orientation

You want new hires to see the selling manager as their supervisor, not a sort of boss/sort of peer. Have new reps accompany or listen to the salespeople as they interact with customers and sell.

Structure their time with the selling sales manager to revolve mainly around supervisory duties like coaching or reviewing the sales reports. Avoid having the new hire see them in the sales role for a period of time.

## Leadership opportunities

Having an experienced salesperson leading the sales staff elevates the department. Navigating the difficulties involved in this dual position and making it a success story could potentially take your company or division to another level. This bodes well for you from an image and career standpoint.

## Summary checklist

### The selling sales manager review and checklist

- Clarify problem.
- Structure the position:
  - Write job description
  - Assess the rep
  - Select account list
  - Conduct the interview process
- Speak with other salespeople.
- Set expectations with department leaders.
- Mentor new selling sales manager.

# Resolution

Alisa couldn't miss the smirk on the marketing director's face. He was inquiring about her progress on the new sales proposal. Weeks ago, he'd e-mailed her three templates and asked for her feedback. She knew exactly what she wanted—a combination of the first and the third. She just didn't have the time to get to it.

Recently, Louis at Tribeqq asked John to take her off the account. For the past several years she had given Louis over-the-top service, dropping everything when he called and seeing to anything he needed. He had gotten used to being her top priority. Now he had to share her time. He wasn't happy.

Then Rebecca walked in. Alisa told her, unleashing weeks of frustration, to start solving her own problems. Rebecca gave her a cool look and walked out of her office.

Later that day, she and John sat in his office, talking the whole situation over. She told him she really enjoyed managing the reps, but just wasn't sure she was doing it correctly. She had tried for months to do both jobs and just couldn't anymore. The two of them started discussing what needed to change.

First, they cut her account list by 25 percent. John volunteered to speak to the customers and reps involved. For the next two weeks, they decided she would stop managing, focusing instead on her remaining customers and trying to make things right.

Next, they agreed to call on Louis together, tell him about her new position, and work out a plan so he felt he was getting the attention he needed. Rebecca suggested a customer service rep dedicated to Tribeqq might help the situation.

She mentioned her struggles with Rebecca and Vince. Having been there himself, he gave her some insightful tips on managing these challenging personalities.

Alisa told John she needed training. About a month ago, she had e-mailed him three links for sales management training companies. He agreed to look them over and make a decision by the end of the week.

The next day, Alisa apologized to Rebecca for losing her temper. Rebecca accepted her apology and began asking for help on a deal she was working on. Remembering John's advice, Alisa interrupted her and said, "Walk me through how you'd handle it if I weren't here. What would your first step be?"

Rebecca looked surprised. She made a few halting remarks and then left Alisa's office. Alisa knows she'll be back. But she now knows how to better control the situation. She almost can't wait until Vince rolls his eyes again.

# Chapter 11
# The Superstar Sales Manager

Well-liked by customers, admired by the sales staff, and undeniably the most talented rep the company had ever hired, it made perfect sense to offer superstar salesperson Phil the position of sales manager.

When company president Vic announced Phil's promotion, the sales staff burst into spontaneous applause. No one clapped louder than Haley. Always an admirer of his sales abilities, she couldn't wait to work more closely with Phil and learn from him.

Now she shakes her head in disbelief while sitting in a client's waiting room. Phil paces up and down the hallway, talking to one of his former clients on the phone. He'll end the conversation just as her customer comes out to greet them. During the sales call, he'll either dominate the conversation or sit by passively. As they walk back to the car, he'll get back on his cell phone.

Phil makes a call immediately after leaving the client's lobby. Disappointed with the way Haley handled the sales call, he picked up his phone to avoid losing his temper. All the reps he now manages rush into their sales presentations before asking enough questions to understand the customer's needs. This baffles him.

As time goes by, the reps avoid taking him on sales calls whenever possible. He mentions an emergency with one of his former clients. They "insist" he see to that instead, assuring him they'll be fine on their own.

Most of the reps stay quiet about the whole situation, except Evan, who took on the majority of Phil's accounts. Vocal when it comes to this situation, he talks about Phil's constant interference with his customers, how the other reps view him, and his disastrous behavior on sales calls.

Eventually, Evan confronts Vic. What Evan has to say surprises him. Vic and Phil have always enjoyed a close relationship. When they talk, Phil assures him he loves the job. What's happening?

Though he hasn't told Vic, Phil can't stand being sales manager and regrets accepting the position. His accounts reassigned to other reps, his updated profile posted to the company Website and social media, a PR release sent to the local business journal—he has no idea what to do.

---

### Problem summary
Former superstar sales rep and new sales manager
- Accepted promotion to sales manager
- Dislikes the position
- Struggles with relating to the reps
- Won't let go of former clients
- Doesn't know what to do

Sales reps
- Looked forward to learning from the new sales manager
- Are disappointed and confused by his management style

- Receive no coaching or guidance from him
- Dread bringing him along on sales calls

Company president

- Thought promotion was the right move
- Transitioned customers to other reps
- Believed sales manager enjoyed his new role
- Is puzzled that things aren't working out

So, the solution is easy, right? As Phil's boss, you have a heart-to-heart with the former superstar salesperson, now sales manager, he acknowledges disliking the job, and you put him right back into his former position. Mission accomplished.

If only it were that simple. For several reasons, retracting the promotion and handing his accounts back might not work. This problem has several layers of complexity:

- Sales managers in this conundrum sometimes go to great pains to convince bosses and supervisors that they enjoy a role they actually despise. Being superstar salespeople, they know about persuasion and disguising their emotions.

- Companies often reorganize or hire new reps to replace the superstars. These new reps often accept the job based on a particular territory assignment or list of accounts.

- Sometimes former superstars take the position under duress. The company might be downsizing, changing their account list, or altering the compensation plan to reduce commissions or bonuses.

- Lastly, superstars become bored with their sales job. Yes, it happens. They need a new challenge, but accept the wrong position: sales manager. They dislike their new role, but can't or won't go back to the old one.

# Getting started

Prior to making any more changes, understand the difference between the qualities of a superstar salesperson versus a sales manager. Read blog posts, books, and magazine articles devoted to the topic.

This chart illustrates the differences and potentially difficult (if not impossible) transition between the two positions.

| Superstar Salespeople | Sales Managers |
|---|---|
| Consistently positive and upbeat | Motivate others |
| Set their own goals | Responsible for achieving company goals |
| Intensely loyal to customers | Represent company's interests |
| Ask high-value questions | Coach reps to ask high-value questions |
| Understand customer needs before presenting | Observe as reps present |
| Have longer tenures with companies | Change jobs more frequently |
| Enjoy the thrill and recognition of winning | Let reps shine, taking little credit |

More than any other skills, the majority of superstars lack the coaching and developing mindset. When managing, they have to focus on someone else, helping that rep rather than making themselves look good. It just doesn't come naturally to them.

Think about your former superstars' relationships with you, their clients, and their coworkers. Due to their high sales revenue production, everyone at the company knows and treats them with some deference. Managers have a peer-like rapport with these reps, granting them more autonomy than the average salesperson on the team.

What about their professional relationships with fellow reps? Most superstars get along fine with their sales teammates, but don't exactly consider them peers. They keep slightly apart from the group.

Unless asked directly by a supervisor, most avoid helping new hires. They lack the time, talent, or interest in that activity. Superstars struggle to put into words how they do what they do.

After considering all this, most company leaders see why this well-intentioned promotion has such little chance of succeeding.

## Create a plan

Former superstar sales reps promoted into sales management fall into three categories:

- Doing a poor job, but doesn't realize it
- Dislikes the job and wants out
- Shows promise, but doesn't know how to do the job

This dilemma calls for two separate approaches: one for the non-performers and/or those wanting to leave the position and one for the former superstar with potential.

## Assessments

No matter which category they fall into, as a first step, administer a sales management assessment. This instrument provides an unbiased, independent view of former superstars' management capabilities, allowing both parties to see where their strengths and weaknesses lie. You engage in a more fact-based, balanced, and less emotional conversation.

## Scenario I (underperforming/dislikes job)

In either case, this former superstar needs to be removed from the role. Because they didn't get themselves into this mess all on their own, it remains incumbent upon company leaders to work with them to find a way out of this conundrum.

Certainly you could reassign *a limited number* of their old accounts back to them. Sincere apologies and explanations smooth most situations over. That won't solve the entire problem, though. You still face compensation or boredom issues.

Most need a new or different challenge. Some suggestions for this include:

- Prospecting for new accounts exclusively
- Making contacts in new industries
- Developing a presence in foreign markets

Before talking to the rep, make sure these ideas have a strong chance of being approved. Understand the options and compromises available. Don't add more disappointments to this situation.

## Scenario II (shows promise)

Regardless of their level of interest in the position, if the assessment shows they lack the skills or abilities to manage people, proceed as you would in the other scenario. Ultimately, this rep won't succeed in the role.

If superstars score well and seem to genuinely enjoy the job, look into a formal training program, followed by some one-on-one coaching.

## Present the plan to executives

When addressing an audience like a CEO or board of directors, review some of the history behind this person accepting the position to begin with. Then talk about the different skills needed to succeed in these two very different roles. Some sophisticated and experienced businesspeople believe superstar reps make superstar sales managers.

Present the assessment results, providing a copy for each person present. Discuss the reasons behind assessing the rep to begin with. If the superstar rep scored on the low side, be open about that.

For the sales managers in denial/disliking the job, review the problems they're experiencing. If the former superstar was forced or maneuvered into the position, say so. Several executives might have had a hand in this promotion. Present alternatives for utilizing their talents and stress the importance of having them remain with the organization.

Where the former superstar shows promise, share your own observations of their performance in the role. Both talk about and recommend the formal sales management training and coaching you've looked into.

# Recruitment

Don't end the meeting without discussing the topic of hiring a new sales manager. At least preliminarily, talk about getting the process started. For company leaders serious about retaining the superstar rep, I recommend conducting that search very discreetly or waiting until after you've assigned the superstar to another role.

## Address the issue with the rep

Although the outcome might be the same, prepare for three different types of conversations with the former superstar rep.

## The "in denial" superstar

Treat this initial talk as an opportunity to learn. If they seem happy in the position, ask questions like:

- You've been in the role for several months now. What do you think?
- What's the biggest difference between sales and management?
- How do you structure your time?

Try not to push an agenda or lead the conversation. Don't expect the former superstar to break down under questioning and admit to disliking managing reps. That probably won't happen—at least not during this talk. If you hear a lot of "Great. Super. Really enjoying myself. I wished I'd started managing years ago," resist digging for more specifics.

Next, without placing blame or expressing disappointment in their performance, get their thoughts on:

- Contacting former customers.
- Accompanying reps on sales calls.
- Managing the sales staff.

Ask open-ended questions and let them talk. Be satisfied with a few more details about their thoughts on the situation. You might find out a few things you hadn't known before.

## The "dislikes the job" superstar

This conversation has both easier and more difficult parts to it. Superstars get used to winning. Even when admitting to the mistake of accepting the management position, they experience a sense of failure as well as anger if pushed into the job.

You try to get the "in denial" superstar to see reality. The "dislikes the job" superstar already does. Outline some of the potential ideas you came up with for new positions. Ask about any suggestion they might have. Listen, but don't push for a resolution. Give them the opportunity to think it over. Don't compound the problem by putting them in another ill-suited role.

## The "shows promise" sales manager

In this case, the former superstar seems to enjoy the new responsibilities and the assessment shows they have the ability to succeed in the role. Without the benefit of sales management training, they might struggle with structuring the job.

Inquire about how they:

- Schedule their time.
- Run the staff meetings.
- Interact with reps.
- Review sales reports.
- Coach and offer support to reps.

Find out:

- What they like best about their new role.
- Where they feel like they're struggling.

Finally, bring up the topic of the differences between the two roles. I advise executives to look for the former superstar to make realistic, mature observations about how the two jobs differ. If they do so, you should feel more comfortable about keeping them in the sales management position.

## Follow-up meeting with the "in denial" superstar

Get underway by asking for their thoughts on the previous conversation. Some may act clueless again, whereas others begin to speak candidly about the situation. No matter which side they come down on, direct the conversation toward the issues.

Former superstar or not, you're disappointed in this new manager's job performance. Yet these chats cannot continue indefinitely. If this situation drags on unaddressed, reps quit, customers buy from other vendors, and sales revenue decreases.

Say to them, "I'm not seeing the results I wanted to when you accepted the position. The reps seem to be struggling with you in the new role as well. I'm particularly concerned about excessive contact with your former accounts, your actions when accompanying the reps on sales calls, and your overall structuring of the job."

## Maintaining contact with former accounts

Former superstars struggle with letting go of clients. Because these accounts generate a lot of sales revenue, many feel they're acting in both the account's and the company's best interests by keeping in touch. Ask about their thoughts with regard to keeping in contact and hear them out.

Show them Evan's most recent notes about *his own* customer, detailing a situation where Phil clearly took on Evan's responsibilities. Find out why.

| Date | Time | Notes | Rep |
|---|---|---|---|
| 18-Aug | 3:19pm | Spoke w/ Cindy. Needs quote on additional licenses | Evan |
| 19-Aug | 8:05am | Called Dan. Contracts in process | Evan |
| 22-Aug | 10:40am | Followed up with Cindy. Phil emailed the updated contract | Evan |
| 30-Aug | 3:19pm | Cindy sent contract back to Phil. Says everything is fine | Evan |

Hear them out, but be clear that except for extenuating circumstances, they no longer have sales responsibility for any account. Explain that customer contact now goes through the rep. Talk about the need for them to step back.

## Accompanying reps on sales calls

To avoid pitting the reps against the former superstar, take all the comments from the salespeople and look for commonalities. If several of them have said almost the exact same thing, combine their comments and say, "The reps tell me that your presence during sales calls make them uncomfortable—you either say nothing or too much. They also tell me you're on the phone almost constantly before and after every call. What's that about?"

Some might get defensive, whereas others put forth a logical explanation. Listen and let the conversation play out. Start a conversation about their role during a joint sales call with a rep.

## Share the facts

At this point, review the results of the sales assessment. Have a frank talk about why people with their profile struggle in a supervisory role. Let them know that to succeed, they'll need to work harder than others more suited to the job. Compare some of their recent behavior with findings in the reports.

In this case be clear their sales career, though spectacular, earns them no more goodwill. To date, their sales management performance falls short of expectations and they must make significant changes.

> Quick tip: When any sales rep scores poorly on a sales management assessment, do not sign them up for formal training right away. Training doesn't fix a lack of skills. Candidates need to acknowledge the situation and do some work on their own first.

## Put the issue in writing

Sometimes, "in denial" superstars come away from conversations understanding what company leaders want them to *stop* doing, but not understanding what they *should* be doing. They might not know exactly what a sales manager does.

How can that be, you wonder? For one thing, superstars tend to excel early in their career. They work hard, but don't struggle to improve their sales skills the way their less-talented peers do. Their more autonomous relationship with their managers leaves them with less of an understanding of the mechanics of the job.

Before moving forward, ask them to pick out a book on sales management and order a copy for each of you. Read it and discuss several chapters at a time. Don't stretch this out. You need to get this situation under control. Complete the book within two weeks.

Once you feel confident that they have a better understanding of the workings of the position, ask them to put a plan in writing.

---

To:        (President)
From:      (Sales manager)
Date:      November 4, 2xxx
Re:        Sales management goals

-----------------------------------------------------------------------------

After discussions with [president's name] as well as hearing how reps and customers feel about my performance as sales manager, I know I need to make some changes. The job of salesperson and the job of sales manager are very different. During the next three months I will do the following:

**Schedule weekly one-on-one meetings with each sales rep to:**

- Understand their goals
- Discuss and observe their strengths and weaknesses
- Work with them in areas needing improvement
- Review their pipelines and forecasts
- Schedule joint customer visits
- Discuss each person's role before the visits
- Offer critiques afterward

**Meet with other managers and directors to:**

- Learn about their goals
- Understand how sales interacts with their department
- Find out how sales can offer support

**Work directly with the vice president of human resources to:**

- Select a management mentor within the company
- Learn about coaching techniques

**Hold weekly staff meetings to:**

- Select a book on sales and discuss a chapter at each meeting
- Use role play exercises to improve sales skills such as: addressing objections and asking effective qualifying questions

**Cease communication with former accounts:**

- If the client initiates call, have the rep get in touch with them
- When problems occur, brainstorm for solutions with the reps

**Meet weekly with [company president] to:**

- Discuss performance of top 10 accounts in each rep's territory
- Review rolled-up forecast
- Read and discuss 2nd book on sales management

_____          _____

Sales manager                    President

Company X                        Company X

Company leaders need to put in the time with the former superstar, meeting frequently and serving as an example. Send out an agenda before every meeting. Hold them accountable to the plan you both signed and agreed to. More than anything else act as a mentor. As company leader, you've managed people for years. Share some of your early supervisory experiences—both the good and the bad. Provide helpful tips. New sales managers remember and appreciate it.

By the end of the first month, most company leaders know whether or not the former superstar has a chance of succeeding as a manager. If it seems to be working, enroll them in a formal sales management training course. They will be receptive to and gain a good deal from the instruction.

If the situation continues to go downhill, you really have no choice but to put them on probation. In conjunction with that action, continue thinking about an alternative position for them within the organization.

## Final meeting (with "dislikes the job" sales manager)

In this case, former superstars want to vacate the position—the sooner the better. They have no interest in a performance improvement plan, giving it another try, or reading a book on sales management. They're ready to go; the details just need to be worked out.

Usually, the plan becomes a combination of reassuming responsibility for a few former customers and opening up a new market. The sticking point commonly revolves around compensation.

Perhaps the company can't or won't pay them what they used to earn. Maybe they gave the sales role up voluntarily. Regardless, the company only stands to benefit if they use their considerable skills to open up a new market. In an effort to retain them, offer the most generous compensation package possible.

With their prior track record of success, the likelihood of failure seems minimal. Consider future revenue from this new market and make a commensurate offer.

> Quick tip: With both the "in denial" and "dislikes the job" rep during any conversation, take the opportunity to acknowledge past contributions. They were stellar salespeople and this has been a tough situation. Say something like, "When you got the signed contract from Bluestone Software, it took the company to another level. I'll always remember and appreciate that."

## Current staff

Unfortunately, no matter how hard company leaders try, a combination of embarrassment, pride, ego, and financial necessity may result in the superstar, regrettably, resigning from both the position and the company. When this happens, call a meeting with the sales team and make a very respectful announcement. This person closed a lot of great deals for the organization. Wish them well in their next endeavor.

Should they choose to stay and accept a newly created role, handle the situation tactfully. Some of the reps might be upset about having a few accounts taken back from them, others disappointed in the lousy job the former superstar did as sales manager.

No matter how uncomfortable, make the announcement to the group with the former superstar present. Work together on what to say. Make a statement such as, "For a long time now, the company has seriously considered pursuing the sustainable energy market. Currently, we have no real presence there. Phil has graciously agreed to help us get established in that market. He'll call on a select group of former accounts as well. That means Phil no longer serves as sales manager. I know all of you join me in wishing him well with this new endeavor."

Let the reps know you'll serve as interim sales manager during the search for a new one. Offer to answer any questions or go into greater detail, if necessary, during individual meetings. One or more of the reps might be interested in the sales management position.

# Hiring

Because you promoted a current employee into the sales management position, you might have made assumptions about their abilities. Maybe you skipped putting together a hiring process. Did informal chats replace formal interviews?

Give the position of sales manager some thought. Understand what it takes to succeed in the role. Have applicants take a sales management assessment to determine their suitability for the job.

Prior to starting the interview process, create:

- A job description.
- 30-, 60-, 90-day goals.
- Strategic initiatives for the year.

Get input from and allow reps to participate in the selection process this time around. Have them meet the applicants and solicit their opinion afterward. This helps regain their trust in your ability to choose leaders. Reference Chapter 10 (The Selling Sales Manager) for more information on the interview process.

## New hire orientation

Sales leaders in every industry get the absolute short end of the stick when it comes to any type of training and orientation. Most spend one hour with HR filling out paperwork, then find themselves rushed into meetings with the sales reps.

An important sale, critical to making the month, needs to be closed. With all their experience, maybe they could offer some suggestions? A rep needs to go on warning and even though they've been in the position less than a day, could they sign off on it? And could they quickly review a proposal? Yes, this happens. Most get sucked into a vortex and don't look up for months.

The sales department never slows down. Deals close all the time. Yes, you should expect them to do their job. But fit some reasonable orientation time in between to include:

- Meeting other department managers.
- Product training.
- CRM and software training.
- Reviewing goals and expectations for the first 90 days.

Invest in the new sales manager. Time spent allowing them to learn about the new company and position pays dividends later on.

## Leadership opportunities

Like company leaders all over the world, you made the logical assumption that a superstar rep could easily transition into the role of superstar sales manager. You meant to do the right thing by the company, the former superstar rep, and the sales staff. It just didn't work out.

Removing any valued employee from the wrong role involves sensitivity and diplomacy. Coming up with a suitable replacement position takes creativity and discretion. Showcase your ability to recognize a mistake and put together a plan to make things right for as many parties as possible.

# Summary checklist
## Superstar sales manager review and checklist

- Clarify problem.
- Understand profile of superstar salesperson versus sales manager.
- Attempt to retain this valuable employee.
- Determine whether the sales managers wants to
  - Stay in position
  - Leave position
- Remove or keep the former sales superstar in sales manager role.
- Set measurable goals for superstar remaining in management position.
- Speak with sales staff about the situation.
- Hire replacement sales manager.

# Resolution

During a late Thursday afternoon conversation with Vic, Phil spoke glowingly about managing salespeople. In particular, he mentioned enjoying coaching the reps and working with them to achieve their target goals.

Though Vic had heard quite the opposite from the reps, maybe he didn't have the whole story. Were the reps exaggerating? Did Phil just need more time? Could Phil be holding them to a higher standard and they resent it?

Then on Monday morning, Phil walked back into his office and resigned. He told Vic he would be accepting an offer with another company immediately after their talk. He apologized for taking the position in the first place, but hated being a sales manager and needed to leave.

Vic assured Phil blame rested on both sides and that he very much wanted him to remain with the company. He asked him to hold off on accepting the offer so they could try and work something out. Phil agreed to do that.

Vic cancelled his appointments for the next two days while he and Phil put their heads together. Surprisingly Phil was full of great ideas. He thought relations between sales and sales engineering was terrible and had some ideas about fixing it. He laughed and said, "While I was a disaster with the reps, I know how to talk to them."

He also felt the company was missing the mark by not investigating the alternative energy markets. He had never mentioned it because he thought it would mean taking a huge reduction in pay while he pursued decision-makers at those companies. He estimated it could take a year or more to break into the industry.

Vic asked Phil if he would remain in the sales management position for another few weeks while he approached the CEO and the board of directors about a new position. He made some suggestions as to how Phil could help the reps in the interim.

Phil agreed to stay and called the other company to decline the offer. Both parties were relieved and ready to start work on the new venture.

# Chapter 12
# Loosely Defined Sales Cycle

Each rep on Walt's sales team has a distinct sales cycle. Julie talks about her "eight-step process" from prospecting to close, whereas Lauren tracks (by Walt's last count) at least 18 different steps. Peter just "closes when it feels right." He cannot really define a cycle.

When he was a salesperson, Walt enjoyed the creative aspect of the job. Every one of his peers took a slightly unique approach to working with customers and closing deals. As a manager, he likes working with different personalities.

Considering himself to be more democratic than autocratic, Walt has no interest in stifling his reps' individual styles. At the same time, he believes the lack of a formalized sales process negatively affects the sales team, the company, and his reputation as a sales leader.

All the reps enter and update customer information in the CRM system consistently and accurately. With the exception of Peter, each rep has set up a separate pipeline report to match the steps in their own sales cycle.

Of the three, Julie turns in the most accurate sales forecast. Peter and Lauren frequently under- and overestimate the closing dates for sales. To complicate matters, Walt's boss, Carl, and Lauren have a close professional relationship. Walt knows Lauren has convinced Carl the company has a long, complicated sales cycle.

The ill-defined sales cycle and separate pipeline reports make discussing the progress of a sale and turning in an accurate sales forecast challenging for Walt. Carl and other department leaders feel frustrated that vague closing dates cause difficulty with predicting cash flow and purchasing estimates. This creates tension at department-wide staff meetings.

Fresh from enduring a lecture at Carl's last department meeting about a large deal of Lauren's that has yet to close, Walt knows he has to do something. In his estimation, the real sales cycle consists of eight steps. Formalizing it would mean big changes for the company in many different departments. But how does he go about gaining consensus with the executive board and a very diverse group of reps?

---

**Problem summary**

Sales reps

- Take an individual approach to the job
- Use sales cycles of different steps and lengths
- Submit inaccurate sales forecasts
- Believe the sales cycle is long
- Create independent reports in the CRM

Sales manager

- Enjoys managing different personalities
- Feels reluctant to impose hard and fast rules
- Turns in imprecise sales forecasts
- Needs to standardize the number of steps in the sales cycle
- Must gain consensus across different departments

---

Two hard truths exist in sales:

- Sales leaders managing reps using different versions of the sales cycle experience difficulty communicating with their superiors. Providing consistently inaccurate or vague information about potential deals causes executives to distrust their reporting abilities—a critical sales management skill.
- Reps hide behind long sales cycles to avoid accountability. Their deals slip between the cracks of steps 5 and 6, pop back up, then get stuck between steps 10 and 11. These reps often lack some of the skills needed to close sales.

Products and services have a natural sales cycle. Though it sometimes takes a while to see it, one exists. Effective managers document and formalize it, then build an accurate reporting system around it.

## Getting started

Prior to making any changes, think about your organization's sales cycle. As a first step, define it as you believe it exists today. Walt believes the real sales cycle follows this sequence:

| |
|---|
| Initial Conversation |
| Second Conversation |
| In-Person Appointment |
| Product Demonstration |
| Appointment w/sales Engineer |
| Proposal |
| Negotiation |
| Close |

Because they sell a technical product, Walt coaches the reps to set up a second phone conversation before trying to schedule an in-person appointment. In his experience, this allows them to ask more discovery questions. When they do meet face-to-face, he believes the decision-maker demonstrates more interest in and commitment to the product.

## The rep's sales cycles

You know each rep's sales cycle—at least anecdotally. Now ask them to write down the steps as a way of formalizing their processes. Make no exceptions, even for the ones who "wing it." Hold them accountable to completing the project.

If they've never had to do this before, some reps struggle with the assignment. Be patient. Give them a chance to explain their thoughts. Don't argue with them or make a case for your sales cycle. Just listen.

## Unexpected benefit

Managers going through this exercise often find, to their surprise, that it provides information to help them more successfully coach reps. As he reviews Lauren's sales cycle, Walt gets a clearer picture of why her deals take so long to close.

| |
|---|
| Company research |
| Determine decision-maker |
| Initial conversation |
| Send e-literature |
| Follow-up |
| Second conversation |
| Identify/speak with influencers |
| Send e-literature |
| Follow-up |
| In-person appointment |
| Follow-up w/ decision-maker |
| Product demonstration |
| Follow-up with decision-maker |
| Mtg. with sales engineer |
| Follow-up |
| Send proposal |
| Negotiate |
| Close |

In the plus column, Lauren builds consensus when she sells. More than any other rep on his team, she takes the time to identify and include the influencers within an organization, respecting their importance in the sales process. Walt sees other reps lose deals when they don't recognize or take influencers seriously. That doesn't happen to Lauren.

In the negative column, Lauren avoids asking the questions necessary to move the deal forward. When he accompanies her on in-person visits, Walt prompts her to schedule another meeting or get some type of commitment while in front of the decision-maker. She resists this.

Seeing the separate steps in her sales cycle written down confirms Lauren's tendency to avoid confrontation. She keeps all face-to-face contact pleasant and product-focused. Then she returns to the office, attempting to further the sale via the phone or e-mail.

Walt reviews each rep's sales cycle, gaining a real insight into how they approach the job. Staff-wide, he notices a pattern of avoiding what they see as confrontation and he views as appropriately moving the sale forward. He feels confident they can address this problem together.

> Quick tip: Companies sometimes have different types of reps within the sales department who cover different types of accounts: national, major, key, government, or education. These reps might have different sales cycles than geo-focused account reps.

## Create a plan

If the reps defined the sales cycle differently, but forecasted sales with great accuracy, sales leaders would likely tackle another more pressing problem first. But that's not the situation here—and it isn't for most companies.

Organizations with an ill-defined sales cycle and an incompatible suite of sales reports experience difficulties with moving deals along and forecasting closing dates correctly.

Document the number of steps in each rep's sales cycle, the length of time it takes them to close a sale (from the first appointment to close), and the percentage of deals leading to closed sales.

| Rep | #Steps | Length of Sales Cycle (Days) | Closed / Won |
|---|---|---|---|
| Lauren | 18 | 83 | 44% |
| Peter | 4 | 60 | 59% |
| Julie | 8 | 51 | 72% |

Many managers discover reps with the longest, most complex sales cycle take the longest amount of time to close deals. Often, they have the lowest percentage of closed opportunities.

Review all the data. Consider what you've learned and which suspicions have been confirmed. Assemble the information and present it to your manager.

## Present the plan to executives

In this situation, the president complains about a problem (inaccurate sales reporting), but might not make the connection between that and a loosely defined sales cycle. Sales leaders need to make a case for one (defining the sales cycle), before agreeing to try and fix the other (inexact sales reports).

During the conversation with your boss, present the various documents you've put together. Review the steps in your suggested sales cycle. Talk about what led you to this discovery. Discuss the correlation between the sales cycle and the sales forecast. Get specific about the problems it causes.

I often recommend using a graph like the one on the next page to emphasize a point when discussing a challenging problem with the reps. In this situation, your boss might benefit as well. Illustrate the difference between your suggested sales cycle and a rep with a particularly lengthy process.

Without criticizing the rep or personalizing the situation, you'll make your point. Leaders see an unwieldy sales cycle in need of editing and refining.

## Bringing others in

Companies need a defined sales cycle for a number of reasons. But a change like this doesn't just affect sales. Marketing or finance (among other departments) will have their own opinions. Some might want to play a role in naming the different stages. Altering the sales cycle could affect lead generation or shared CRM reporting, for example.

Fixing this problem involves bringing different departments together. Before opening this topic up to a discussion with other company leaders, reach agreement with your supervisor about the necessity of formalizing the sales cycle. Discuss handling potential pushback from the other department managers.

| Walt's sales cycle | Lauren's sales cycle |
|---|---|
| Initial conversation | Company research |
| Second conversation | Determine decision maker |
| In-person appointment | Initial conversation |
| Product demonstration | Send e-literature |
| Appointment w/ sales engineer | Follow-up |
| Proposal | Second conversation |
| Negotiate | Identify/speak with influencers |
| Close | Send e-literature |
| | Follow-up |
| | In-person appointment |
| | Follow-up w/ decision-maker |
| | Product demonstration |
| | Follow-up with decision-maker |
| | Mtg. with sales engineer |
| | Follow-up |
| | Send proposal |
| | Negotiate |
| | Close |

You need your boss's complete support. Don't end up with a *slightly* better version of the sales cycle than what you deal with now. You're the sales expert. Be open to compromise, but insist on one that represents the real sales pattern.

## The sales forecast

Reaching consensus on the sales cycle enables sales leaders to address the problems and complaints about the sales forecast (a document made up of those deals the reps expects to close within 30, 60, or 90 days).

With the reps using all different steps and names in their individual sales cycles, Walt struggled to turn in uniform sales forecasts. In his opinion, no deal should appear on the sales forecast until the decision-maker has participated in the product demonstration (step #4 under Walt's sales cycle).

Going forward, the entire sales staff will know that only those potential clients successfully completing step #4 can be considered for the monthly sales forecast.

## Address the issue with the rep

In some cases, sales leaders could limit the discussion of a formalized sales cycle to just the reps. No one else might need to be involved. Let's say salespeople on the team use a sales process with either four, five, or six steps, which they realize creates problems. After some compromise and discussion, they reach agreement on a five-step sales cycle.

Sales leaders could discuss the new sales cycle with their supervisor and other executives, get approval, adjust the reporting, and move forward.

On a staff where this issue creates problems (and has for some time) and the reps use widely variant sales cycles (or none at all), I believe sales executives must take the lead. They need to present and make a case for a consistent sales cycle to be used by all reps.

Once you gain consensus with your boss and all other appropriate parties, schedule one-on-one discussions with the salespeople. List the problems and the challenges that having different sales cycles creates from both your perspective and that of other department leaders.

Unveil the new sales cycle. Explain the various observations, discussions, and experiences that led you to determine the separate steps in the process. Consider the rep's perspective.

Independent by nature, most salespeople dislike a lot of formalization, process, and procedure. They resist change. Altering the sales cycle involves using different language and creating new CRM reports. Compensation comes to mind right away for most. Reps wonder, "How will this new sales cycle affect the amount of money I am able to earn?"

Removing the rep's name, show the sales staff the same chart you showed your boss. Explain the thought process behind your suggested sales cycle. Listen to what they have to say.

Reps with many more steps than necessary in their sales cycles often confuse administrative duties (and the endless follow-up involved in the profession of sales) with major milestones or progress in closing a deal.

As an example, when reps conduct pre-call research, it helps them have an educated conversation with a decision-maker. It doesn't represent a separate step in the process. Go over their sales cycles individually and point out where you see discrepancies.

Make clear that you believe a sales cycle with fewer steps:

- Shortens the length of time from cold calling to close.
- Separates the suspects from the prospects.
- Focuses their energies on deals with greater potential.
- Ultimately increases their earnings.

Emphasize a common sales cycle creates a uniform way to: have conversations, provide support (like which marketing materials to use during a particular phase), and offer coaching.

## Reluctant reps

Be prepared for some reps to defend their sales cycle vigorously. They'll passionately fight to maintain the status quo.

Have specific examples at the ready. Remind reps about deals that languished in between the various steps in their sales cycle for a long time—never closing. Refresh their memory about the hours spent with these prospects and the emotional toll of not getting a signed contract.

Say something along the lines of, "Let's look at The McCafferty Group. This company spent nine months moving from one step in your sales cycle to the next. I see in the CRM, you still follow up with them every few weeks. Think of the energy you've spent on this. You've yet to do business with them."

As you did with the company president, show them the chart with their individual sales cycle versus the one you feel represents the actual process.

## Current staff

After you've spoken with all reps one-on-one, meet with the entire staff. Present the new sales cycle. Review any changes involved, including sales forecasting and CRM reports.

I advise sales leaders dealing with this issue to invite the other executives involved to this staff meeting. The reps know where you stand. Ask different department leaders to speak. Let the reps hear from others how a formalized sales cycle helps them do their job more effectively.

Keep the overall tone of the meeting positive and collaborative. The reps operated with individual sales cycles for quite some time. Don't place blame. Stress company growth and continuous improvement. All companies make changes to better their processes.

End the meeting by telling them you know they don't all agree with or embrace the new sales cycle. Assure them you took notes about their individual opinions during the one-on-ones. Ask them to work with the new sales cycle, as is, for one business quarter.

After the quarter ends, let them know you'll meet with them individually and as a group, along with the executive committee, to assess the new sales cycle. You'd be open to considering potential changes at the point, but not before.

## Improving skills

High-performing sales reps take risks by asking certain key questions at different phases of the sales cycle such as, "You've told me you're seriously considering three vendors at this point. Where does my company rank among those three?"

They listen carefully to the answers, ask more probing questions, and encourage customer objections. Solid information allows them to move a deal forward or alerts them to a problem.

Reps with long sales cycles tend to avoid asking hard questions. They often want to please the customer and then hope some of the business comes their way.

Select an appropriate sales book addressing this issue (or whatever issue you've found to be part of the problem). Ask the reps to read one chapter before every sales meeting. Have a different rep lead the discussion each week.

## Manage to the sales cycle

Use staff meetings to brainstorm with the reps. Make a list of questions that need to be asked before a deal qualifies for the next step in the sales cycle. Take turns having the reps play the buyer and the seller for role-play exercises.

Let the reps know that when they move a prospect from one step in the sales cycle to the next, you'll be asking them for the answers to those questions. If they don't have the information, the prospect cannot move to the next step.

# Hiring

Reps without consistent procedures in any area—cold calling, addressing objections—struggle with achieving their full potential. The same goes for the sales cycle.

Ask all applicants about the sales cycle with their current employer:

- Can they articulate the different steps?
- Do all the reps adhere to the same sales process?
- How is it used in sales reporting?

During interviews, mention the defined sales cycle. Talk about the separate steps getting incorporated into sales reporting, policies, and interdepartmental communication. When candidates meet with other employees, have them bring the subject up as well.

Hire only those who understand the importance of a consistent, company recognized sales cycle.

# New hire orientation

Going forward, new hires enter a stable situation with a systematized sales cycle used by the reps. All sales reports reflect the new steps. Management and the reps use more of the same language.

During the early weeks of their tenure, refer to the sales process often. Monitor their actions to ensure consistency with the new sales cycle.

# Leadership opportunities

Whether you manage three reps or oversee a division with 100 salespeople, you can't have everybody running off in different directions. It doesn't work well for the company and calls into question your management abilities. Recognizing individuality differs from chaos.

Sales leaders in this situation need to prove their case, bring people together, mediate, set boundaries, and ultimately change culture. Those able to do it show themselves to be forward thinking, consensus builders, and developing cohesion between different departments. What a great reputation to have.

## Summary checklist
### Loosely defined sales cycle review and checklist
- Clarify problem.
- Document each rep's sales cycle.
- Create accurate sales cycle.
- Present new sales cycle to boss.
  - Enlist their support with other departments
- Speak with reps.
  - Announce changes
- Update forecasting approach.
- Coach reps.
- Monitor adherence to new sales cycle.

## Resolution

Right after the meeting about the new sales cycle, Lauren follows Carl into his office. Walt hears their raised voices behind closed doors for quite some time. Even though it makes him angry and uncomfortable, he was ready for this.

Later, Carl approached Walt with a new sales cycle—a compromise between Walt's version and Lauren's. Walt stood his ground, showing Carl the various charts and graphs again. He spoke candidly about some of the weaknesses in Lauren's approach to sales and reemphasized the sales forecast problems.

"I don't see how I can turn in a more accurate sales forecast using Lauren's unwieldy sales cycle. I need your support on this," he said. Carl apologized and told Walt to move forward with the originally agreed-upon sales cycle.

Once she had to start working within the confines of the new sales cycle, Lauren experienced a lot of difficulty. Although Walt's working hard to coach her on when to move accounts into which phase of the new sales cycle, he's not sure she can do it. In the next few months he expects she'll resign or he'll need to put her on warning.

Though not happy about the possibility of losing a long-time sales rep like Lauren, Carl now sees the problems her long sales cycle causes when she turns in her sales forecast. He fully supports Walt. The increased accuracy in the forecasts Walt turns in has improved their working relationship immensely. Each has a better understanding of the pressures the other faces in their respective jobs.

# Chapter 13
# The Mediocre Rep

Five years. That's how long she's sat in his office talking about the latest novel her book group selected and asking for advice on sales matters.

For director of sales Jeremy, these chats with salesperson Anne, a very pleasant person, have become increasingly annoying. During the first few years, he thought he could motivate her to excel. Despite all his coaching and guidance, though, she continues to struggle with overcoming objections and reading buying signs from decision-makers.

In eight years with the company, she has always hit her annual sales goal, but only by 1 or 2 percent. When other reps struggle with bad months or quarters, she stays consistent. Customers never complain about her. When Jeremy hires new reps, he has them work with Anne first.

Jeremy thinks about Connor, two years with the company, now trending at 140 percent of quota. Anne trained him. Most new reps surpass her within a year or so.

If she performed at the group average (112 percent), her sales revenue would increase by several hundred thousand dollars. Instead, she remains in her comfort zone, closing deals of a certain size and just making quota.

Anne's average sales numbers combined with one rep not making quota sometimes puts Jeremy's quarter or year-end in jeopardy. For the hundredth time, he wonders whether it's smarter to remain with the status quo (Anne) or replace her to try and improve the situation.

---

### Problem summary

Sales rep

- Just meets quota every year
- Struggles with basic sales concepts
- Needs a lot of management support
- Avoids larger customers and sizeable deals

Director of sales

- Enjoys the rep as a person
- Coaches her on the same sales skills repeatedly
- Frustrated as the other reps with less experience surpass her
- Loses sales revenue and market share in her territory

---

Oh, the mediocre salesperson, so frustrating to deal with. Sales leaders all over the world, in every industry, spend countless hours listening to, coaching, and trying to motivate this rep. They want desperately to figure out the one idea, thought, or phrase that motivates them to get to the next level.

Mediocre reps close sales, represent the company well, and generally get along with coworkers. They avoid the peaks and valleys that other reps experience; their steady production occasionally saving the month or quarter.

Yet, as other salespeople realize 30 to 40 percent gains or higher, this vexing rep comes in right at quota. Relative to their performance, they demand a lot of attention from management, needing support and coaching on the same sales issues again and again.

## Getting started

Take some of the exasperation out of this situation by reviewing the mediocre rep's performance going back as many years as possible.

|  | Quota | Actual | Difference | % + / - |
|---|---|---|---|---|
| Year 1 | $ 1,750,000 | $ 1,764,000 | $ 14,000 | 100.8% |
| Year 2 | $ 1,810,000 | $ 1,832,000 | $ 22,000 | 101.2% |
| Year 3 | $ 1,865,000 | $ 1,939,000 | $ 74,000 | 104.0% |
| Year 4 | $ 1,893,000 | $ 1,889,000 | $ (4,000) | 99.8% |
| Year 5 | $ 1,927,000 | $ 1,945,000 | $ 18,000 | 100.9% |
| Year 6 | $ 1,946,000 | $ 1,989,000 | $ 43,000 | 102.2% |
| Year 7 | $ 1,988,000 | $ 1,973,000 | $ (15,000) | 99.2% |
| Year 8 | $ 2,073,000 | $ 2,099,000 | $ 26,000 | 101.3% |
| Totals | $ 15,252,000 | $ 15,430,000 | $ 178,000 | 101.2% |

With a high of 104 percent and a low of 99.2 percent, you see the rep has always performed like this and nothing you have tried to do has moved the needle on their revenue production one way or the other.

> Quick tip: When puzzled by a rep's actions, I recommend looking at performance reviews and reports written about them by previous managers. Often, those managers reference the same problems you're dealing with. It enables you to look at the problem in a new light and depersonalize the situation. Or, if you kept them, look at notes you made when you interviewed the rep and checked their references.

# Keep a log

In one of the ultimate ironies of business mid-level producers demand the most attention from management. They pursue it aggressively, and often complain loudly if they feel short-changed. Unfortunately, harried, stressed managers voluntarily give these reps more time than they should.

Though counterintuitive, it makes sense. Superstars ask for assistance with tricky, multilayered, multidepartment problems having no easy answer. Working with underperformers involves disappointment, progressive discipline, and termination—all emotional conversations. Average reps usually approach management with solvable problems, and then stay a while to chat. Sometimes these exchanges provide a break from the more stressful aspects of the job.

Without making an attempt to change anything, at least initially, understand how much of your day they take up. Track time spent on phone calls, e-mail, Skype, texting, and face-to-face meetings. Most sales leaders express surprise at the amount of time and energy spent on these reps.

# Territory potential

Most mediocre reps achieve their goals. But with all the same tools at their disposal as anyone else on the sales staff, they lag behind. In year eight, the mediocre rep (Anne) comes in at 15 percent below the group average.

|  | Quota | Actual | Difference | % + / - |
|---|---|---|---|---|
| Julie | $ 2,100,000 | $ 2,675,000 | $ 575,000 | 127% |
| Connor | $ 2,000,300 | $ 2,800,000 | $ 799,700 | 140% |
| Anne | $ 2,073,000 | $ 2,099,000 | $ 26,000 | 101% |
| Nate | $ 2,200,000 | $ 2,100,000 | $ (100,000) | 95% |
| Zachary | $ 2,195,000 | $ 2,544,000 | $ 349,000 | 116% |
| Totals | $ 10,568,300 | $ 12,218,000 | $ 1,649,700 | 116% |

If you'd like to see the cumulative impact of the underperformance, look at the mediocre rep's actual sales performance during the last five years and multiply it by the group average for that same year.

| | Quota | Actual | Group Average | Difference |
|---|---|---|---|---|
| Year 4 | $ 1,893,000 | $ 1,889,000 | 16% | $ 302,240 |
| Year 5 | $ 1,927,000 | $ 1,945,000 | 12% | $ 233,400 |
| Year 6 | $ 1,946,000 | $ 1,989,000 | 9% | $ 179,010 |
| Year 7 | $ 1,988,000 | $ 1,973,000 | 14% | $ 276,220 |
| Year 8 | $ 2,073,000 | $ 2,099,000 | 11% | $ 230,890 |
| Totals | $ 9,827,000 | $ 9,895,000 | 12% | $ 1,187,400 |

In year five, the rep came in at 100.9 percent of quota ($1,927,000/1,945,000). Had she achieved the group average of 12 percent above quota, she would have sold an additional $233,400. Through a period of five years, the company has lost slightly more than one million dollars in sales revenue.

Revenue aside, other losses include lower:

- Commissions for the rep.
- Sales leader bonuses.
- Sales contest cash and prizes.
- Group bonuses.

That one million-plus dollars in sales doesn't disappear, it goes to the competition. Your competitors gain ground in that territory as long as the mediocre rep remains with your organization.

## Assess the rep

Most sales leaders, having spent considerable time with the mediocre reps, generally understand their strengths and challenges. But what other factors might prevent them from improving their sales performance?

If you knew more specifically what held a particular rep back, would it be beneficial? In a situation where reps have tenure of five years or longer, the company has already made a significant investment and commitment.

Spend the money for a sales assessment and see if it yields any valuable information. Undoubtedly, it will.

# Create a plan

Ideally, mediocre reps improve their sales production or get moved out of the organization. Unfortunately, many remain with companies and perform below the group average for years because no mechanism exists to address the situation.

# Set departmental standards

Dealing with this problem involves changes to policy and procedure. Add the following to sales department policies and procedures:

*Sales representatives falling below the group average for two consecutive months will be placed on probation. If a rep falls below the group average for a third month, they must meet with their manager to determine the next course of action—up to and including termination.*

Let's say a rep performs below the group average for two consecutive months, achieves quota the next, and then misses for another two months running. Avoid this management energy drain through the following:

*Should a sales representative fall below the group average for two consecutive months, or twice in the same business year, they will be subject to termination.*

This provides managers with a clear and impartial path for handling this situation.

# Address one area for improvement

If the assessment shows them needing to improve in several key areas, plan to focus on just one initially. Taking on too many sales skills at the same time overwhelms most mediocre reps. Pick a single skill and drill down.

During one-on-one meetings, give them the responsibility of choosing the area they want to work on. Ask them to select a book on the topic. They need to take ownership of the problem and become more independent.

# Change up the interactions

Start owning some of this problem. Mediocre reps have a talent for steering conversations off course and off subject. Even seasoned managers get caught unaware. Begin by taking charge of the one-on-one meetings.

If the two of you normally talk in your office, start meeting in a conference room. If you speak by Skype, use conference calling for a change. If meetings typically take place in the morning, switch to the afternoon. Altering the norm takes people out of their comfort zone and gives you more confidence as you begin to change your management approach.

Prior to all one-on-one meetings, send out an agenda. For example, start off with the book discussion and a review of their assignments. Next, discuss their sales performance against quota and minimum productivity standards like prospecting calls and presentations. Schedule the meeting for a certain amount of time and end it promptly.

When they call or come into your office for help, push back. Say things like:

- We've discussed addressing that objection on several occasions. How have I advised you to respond?
- You and I have talked about buying signals many times. What are you sensing from this decision-maker?

When having yet another time draining conversation you know won't go anywhere, tell them, "I have 10 minutes right now and all the time you need after five."

Enough said. We both know they won't be back at 5:05 p.m.

## Present the plan to executives

CEOs and presidents read the sales reports. They know all too well the rep's history with regard to sales performance.

Review your findings, including: loss of revenue, deals going to the competition, superior performances of reps with far less tenure, and the management time spent on this individual. Stick to the numbers and stay away from personalities. Having been loyal employees of several years standing, these reps probably have a few friends.

Once you've shared this information, open up a discussion about adding or changing current sales policies around this problem. Present suggestions on possible wording for the document.

Mediocre reps rely on and really scream for management support. When you start to pull back, they notice. Few accept the situation quietly; some might go over your head and up the chain of command.

Deal with this potential problem proactively by telling supervisors about the changes you're planning to make in the way you manage this rep. Ask for their support. Remind them that the majority of your time needs to be spent with top producers.

## Address the issue with the rep

Start the first conversation casually. Let them know you only have 15 minutes, but wanted to speak with them. Make a statement along the lines of, "You've been at the company for eight years now. We've both seen some changes. Looking back, why did you choose this company to begin with?"

See how they respond. Then say, "I've been reviewing the sales numbers in a few different ways over the last few weeks. Let's take a look."

Show them the charts detailing their individual performance against quota during their tenure at the company. Ask them, "Did you realize you consistently finish the year between 100 and 104 percent of your annual goal? Why do you think that is?"

When looking at the group average chart, ask, "With everyone having similar sized territories and the same technology at their disposal, why do you think you consistently fall below the group average?"

Practice your new management style right away. If reps switch the subject to a new book they're reading, look at your cell phone or watch and respond with, "I don't mean to interrupt, but we only have a few minutes left. Can you send me the link? I can read about it."

When they look for sales advice, ask, "What would your instinct be if I weren't available?" Listen to their response, schedule a follow-up meeting, then conclude the discussion.

---

Quick tip: In the early phases of changing your interactions with the mediocre reps, schedule any discussions with them for 15 or 20 minutes before a planned conference call or meeting. This helps both you and the reps acclimate to having less of your time, sticking to business, and thinking for themselves.

## Follow-up meeting

Revisit your last conversation by saying, "Did you have a chance to think about our chat a few days ago? What are your thoughts about why you consistently finish in the middle?" Acknowledge what they have to say, and then move on.

Again, change tactics. Stop trying to motivate them. This approach works with other reps, but never with the mediocre rep. Instead of attempting to pump them up, try discussing what they miss out on.

## Lost income

Using the group average, estimate the approximate amount of commissionable sales that have been left on the table during the last five years.

| | Actual | Group Average | Difference | Est. comm. rate | Lost Income |
|---|---|---|---|---|---|
| Year 4 | $ 1,889,000 | 16% | $ 302,240 | 5% | $ 15,112 |
| Year 5 | $ 1,945,000 | 12% | $ 233,400 | 5% | $ 11,670 |
| Year 6 | $ 1,989,000 | 9% | $ 179,010 | 5% | $ 8,951 |
| Year 7 | $ 1,973,000 | 14% | $ 276,220 | 5% | $ 13,811 |
| Year 8 | $ 2,099,000 | 11% | $ 230,890 | 5% | $ 11,545 |
| Totals | $ 9,895,000 | 12% | $ 1,187,400 | 5% | $ 59,370 |

Present the data in visual display form to the rep. This makes an impression that nothing else seems to equal. See what they have to say.

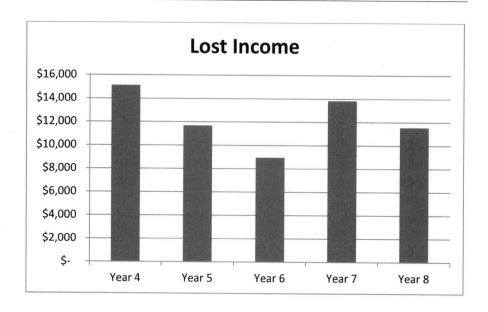

## Review the assessment

Mediocre reps usually score on the low but acceptable side. Although they have the capacity to perform in the role, as evidenced by always just making quota, sales simply doesn't come naturally. They need to work harder than most of their peers to achieve the same results.

Discuss the findings with them. Move ahead with asking *them* to identify and draft a plan for working on one problem area identified by the assessment. Have *them* select a book to read on the topic. Discuss one chapter each week during your one-on-ones. Assign homework.

Should you disagree with the problem area or book they select, don't jump in. Remember to focus on increasing independent thought and action.

## Set goals

Asking this rep to jump from 101 percent or so to 112 percent might never be possible and definitely not doable in the short term. You've come this far with them; stay the course. I recommend that managers in this situation set graduated goals such as:

| Month 1 | Month 2 | Month 3 | Month 4 |
|---------|---------|---------|---------|
| 105%    | 108%    | 110%    | 112%    |

Be clear about your intent. Make sure they understand that remaining in the position of sales representative requires being at or above the group average going forward. Don't defend your actions. Depersonalize the discussion by referring back to the accumulated loss of revenue and market share.

## Put it in writing

When bringing the meeting to a conclusion, ask a final question. "Do you want to get out of the middle of the pack?" With their job in jeopardy, potentially for the first time, they'll likely answer, "Yes." Then ask, "How do you intend to do that?"

Ask them to put their ideas in writing. Refrain from making any suggestions. You've been doing that for years—quarter after quarter. Let them work their own way out of this, based on any feedback you've previously provided.

## Current staff

You have, on your staff, a mediocre producer. Throughout their career, most sales leaders either inherit or hire a rep with this profile at one time or another. Avoid the appearance of singling any one rep out. Handle this problem appropriately through the use of policies and procedures.

Take the time to look at the sales department manual. Do any other policies need to be updated, added, or deleted? If so, request approval from your direct supervisor. Whenever possible, make these changes before having to put mediocre reps on warning (if it comes to that).

Announce any departmental changes during a regular staff meeting. As you did during one-on-ones with the rep in question, discuss loss of revenue and market share as the reason for this. Offer to answer any more specific questions during one-on-one conferences.

End the meeting on a positive note. Get the team focused on and thinking about improving their own averages by creating a sales contest.

Tell the group if they beat their individual monthly average by 5 percent this month, they'll receive a gift certificate to their favorite store.

# Hiring

Superstar and mediocre reps share a commonality: Most perform that way early in their career and don't change. Learn to spot them right away by having all applicants for open sales positions take pre-employment sales assessments.

Those scoring in the average range according to whatever scale the assessment uses should be dropped from consideration. You now know the odds of bringing candidates from average to above average performers.

To support the assessment's findings, ask them to show you recent monthly or quarterly reports showing their rankings within the group. Have them scrub any confidential information. Steer clear of those showing a mid-pack performance.

During the interview process, ask questions like:

- What goals did you set for yourself this year—apart from those set by the company?
- Tell me about the largest deal you've ever closed.
- What do you consider to be your biggest shortcoming in sales and what have you done to address it?

Applicants' answers to these questions help you hire salespeople with drive and ambition above and beyond company expectations.

# New hire orientation

When scheduling their time in the early weeks, have new reps interact with top performers, instead of starting them off with the average producers as you did in the past. Average performers often volunteer and have a talent for this activity. High-achieving reps only train new hires when asked.

Speak with your top performers beforehand. Ask them to share their approach to the job and some of what they've learned along the way.

As new hires begin to make sales calls, look out for mediocre performances early on. If the prospecting goal for month two is 50 calls and they consistently make 50 or 52—in other words just enough but no more—discuss this with them right way. Talk about minimum performance equating to average sales.

Review any and all sales policies and procedures during the orientation period.

## Leadership opportunities

Mediocre reps lower the bar. When they remain in their position for a long period of time, a message gets sent to new hires and tenured reps alike: as a company we tolerate just hitting quota. That's all you really have to do.

By creating new policies around quota achievement, moving reps up or out, and critiquing your own management style, you display a willingness to grow and make hard decisions. Now, you really do direct the sales team.

## Summary checklist
### Mediocre rep review and checklist

- Clarify problem.
- Gather data on:
  - Rep's annual performance against quota
  - Lost revenue within assigned territory
- Present plan to executives.
- Make approved policy additions and changes.
- Ask the rep to create an action plan.
- Set graduated revenue improvement goals.
- Discuss policy changes with the current staff.
- Regularly evaluate the rep's progress.

## Resolution

After their second discussion and review of her assessment scores, Jeremy wondered if Anne would jump right in and try to increase her revenue production. She did not and, to her credit, never made any sort of half-hearted attempt for appearance's sake. She neither selected a book nor bothered to put together an improvement plan.

Just as he was about to put her on warning, he received a call from Catherine in sales fulfillment, asking to interview Anne. Apparently, Anne had expressed interest in Catherine's open lead nurturing management position.

At first, Jeremy was surprised. Would Anne be able to earn the same amount of money? Wouldn't she miss the freedom that sales jobs offer? What about the excitement of closing a deal? Looking at it another way, Jeremy could see her doing a great job of handling the initial conversations with prospects and teaching other sales development reps to do the same. She could easily manage that group.

After meeting with her several times, Catherine offered Anne the job. Jeremy congratulated her enthusiastically. If she needed any advice on managing others, he told her his door was always open. Anne thanked him and promised to let him know about any good books she reads in the future. Jeremy felt relieved and happy about the company retaining a good employee and their parting on good terms.

# Chapter 14
# Unqualified Vice President of Sales

Carl finally built his business up to the point where he felt justified in hiring a salesperson. It was both an exciting and scary time for him. He hired Gina, an experienced rep, for the position. During the interview process, she told him she had been selling for years. She felt ready for a role that included managing future hires and participating in company decisions.

Though she understood her responsibilities would include only sales initially, she asked for the title of vice president of sales. Carl never thought a rep of Gina's caliber would be interested in his small company. Not wanting to lose her over a simple job title, he agreed.

At first, it worked. Gina regularly achieved quota. Carl sought her opinion when it came to sales-related decisions. A veteran salesperson, she offered sound, commonsense suggestions during their discussions.

As the company grew, he hired two additional salespeople, Max and Pauline. Both started to outperform Gina by a solid margin. Though Carl never gave her any formal authority over the two new reps, she acted as if she was their manager. A strained relationship developed among the three of them.

Carl now sees Gina more realistically: a scrappy, solid salesperson, but not vice president of sales material. She lacks the management experience and gravitas to hold the title. He thinks Max has sales management potential.

He knows what he needs to do: give Gina the title of sales rep and offer Max a sales management position. Carl appreciates Gina's contribution to the sales effort. He does not want to embarrass her. He certainly does not want her to quit. He just doesn't know how to go about this.

---

### Problem summary

Vice president of sales

- Is a successful sales rep
- Is a valued employee
- Held the title since the first day on the job
- Lacks managerial experience
- Is the wrong person for the position

Company president

- Regrets giving the rep the title
- Sees the problems it's causing
- Wants to promote another rep to sales manager
- Is concerned about the current VP quitting

---

I see this scenario again and again when meeting with new clients. At some point during our sales related conversations, they might break eye contact with me. Others clear their throat or speak more quietly. Then they start to talk…about their vice president of sales.

Some agreed to give a rep the title without thinking the implications through. Others believed having a VP of sales made the company look larger and more sophisticated. Many worried that if they didn't agree to the title then the talented reps would accept positions elsewhere. And so on.

To most leaders, this decision seemed innocuous at the time. As companies grow, a misapplied title creates genuine problems they never anticipated.

## Getting started

Before taking action, understand the role of vice president of sales. Do a little research. Read a few articles and blogs about the job. Educate yourself on what, exactly, a vice president of sales does. How do their responsibilities differ from a sales rep or a sales manager?

Speak to peers and networking colleagues running companies with VPs of sales on staff. Ask about their hiring process. What was their current VP's prior professional experience? Do they have a sales manager as well? Why or why not?

Many differences exist between reps, managers, and VPs:

- Sales reps work for the customer.
- Sales managers work for the reps and the company.
- VPs of sales work for the company.

Although they are considered the overall head of sales, VPs of sales concentrate, alongside other executives, on overall company performance.

Compare some of the responsibilities among the three positions:

| Salesperson | Sales Manager | VP of Sales |
|---|---|---|
| Represent company to customers | Coach | Develop company sales plan |
| Achieve revenue goal | Motivate | Responsible for revenue production |
| Know product / service | Check sales activity | Plan 12 – 18 months into future |
| Study the competition | Monitor CRM reporting | Recognize, mentor, and deploy talent |
| Cover assigned territory or account list | Hire new salespeople | Visit customers periodically |
| Close new business | Strategize on deals | Hire sales managers |
| Understand customer issues / problems | Visit customers regularly | Monitor activity by teams or sales units |

# Create a plan

Think out 18 months to two years. How do you see the sales department being structured? What major changes might be under consideration? Keeping it all in mind, write job descriptions for the positions as you visualize them for the future.

---

### Sample sales manager job description

The position of sales manager reports directly to the president and involves supervising all sales staff-related efforts.

**Sales revenue**

- Achieve and exceed sales revenue goal through the sales team
- Work with president to set individual and team goals
- Prepare sales forecasts by product and territory
- Track sales team metrics and report data to president on a regular basis
- Collaborate with department leaders on sales related initiatives

---

**Sales representative development**

- Develop direct reports through coaching, motivating, and improving sales skills and product knowledge
- Work with and observe the sales representatives on a regular basis
- Create sales contests to motivate sales reps
- Organize the recruitment effort for new salespeople
- Implement an appraisal system to monitor performance

**Company values**

- Ensure customer satisfaction
- Uphold company vision, values, and policies
- Act as arbiter amongst the salespeople on issues of conflict

Next, create a future organizational chart.

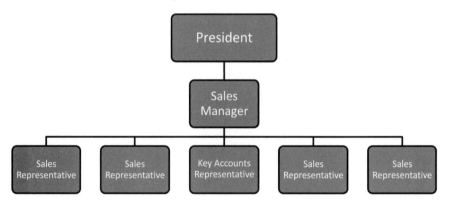

For my clients, completing these two exercises creates some "a-ha" moments. They stop concentrating on one employee—the VP of sales—and one action, giving them a more appropriate title. Instead, they focus on re-organizing the sales department to more appropriately and effectively meet the company's current and future needs.

## Present the plan to executives

If you manage the current VP of sales, you might not have a direct supervisor. You could, however, answer to a board of directors or a venture capital group. They may have some say over your plan.

Before sharing your ideas, review the job descriptions and organizational chart with some trusted advisers, a round table, or peer group. Ask for their opinions and critiques. Make any necessary revisions.

## Address the issue with the rep

Prior to having a conversation with the current VP of sales, think about them as an employee and a sales rep:

- What are their strengths and weaknesses?
- How have they contributed to the organization overall?
- Through the years, has anything about them surprised you— positively or negatively?

If you had to do it all over again, knowing them as you do now, what responsibilities and titles would you give them?

As you jot down your thoughts, some interesting ideas might filter through. Many leaders realize the VP of sales works very effectively with the largest or key accounts. Another understands and relates to the small businesses. Some do a great job of working with new hires. Others know the product or service better than almost anyone at the company.

Identifying the VP's special talents helps you determine their future role. It eases the awkwardness of the conversation ahead.

> Quick tip: All employees have something to offer—above and beyond their day-to-day responsibilities. Everyone enjoys being recognized for their unique contribution.

## The conversation

Begin the talk by sharing a little history. Discuss starting the company. Be candid about the ups and downs you've faced. Recall how nervous you were about hiring them. Share a positive first impression or a specific detail during the initial interview. Listen to anything they have to say.

Steer the conversation toward the future. Say something like, "As you know, I was the company's first sales rep. I hired you and you were the sole rep for a few years. I appreciate you and your many contributions to this company. Recently, I hired Max and Pauline. In the next three years, I want to expand the sales force to five. Doing that involves making changes, including a different role for you."

"I want to change your title to more accurately reflect your contribution to the company—sales representative. Going forward, my plans include having a sales manager overseeing the sales effort. When Max and Pauline first started, I asked you to train them. You did a fantastic job. As we continue to grow, how would you feel about being in charge of new hire orientation?"

Or:

"You handle five of the seven largest accounts in the company. Of the five, you brought in two through prospecting. You have a real talent for working with major accounts. How would you feel about taking on the role of major account sales representative?"

## Stand firm

VPs responses to this upcoming change run the gamut:

- What did I do wrong?
- What do I need to improve to keep the position?
- I took this job to be VP of sales and now you're taking it away?
- Do you know what I've done for this company?
- I can't believe this.
- Some sit in stunned silence.

Take a share of the blame right up front. One of my clients, facing this same situation (with a *family member* no less), said to the current VP, "I gave you the title of vice president of sales before I had a clue what a vice president of sales actually did."

Allow them to vent. Answer their questions. Acknowledge mistakes. Stress the fact that you built a company with little understanding of how to structure a sales department. Keep the conversation focused on the future.

Knowing her better a few years later, you see her as a real contributor, just in a different role.

> Quick tip: Company leaders imagine the current VP quitting right on the spot and convincing many of their best customers to move with them to a new employer.
>
> Though they might quit eventually, it usually doesn't happen immediately. Especially if they weren't job hunting, it's unlikely they'd have another position lined up. They have bills to pay just like everyone else. Do what you can preemptively to protect yourself prior to having the conversation.

## Various reactions

The title of vice president of Sales carries prestige. Those words appear on your current VP's business card. The Website identifies her as such. She introduces herself to clients that way. Family and friends know it as her title. No one—no matter how unqualified—willingly gives that up.

This change represents a demotion and loss of status; it's an embarrassment. The whole situation forces them to take a hard look at their talents and career.

Be prepared for them to take the rest of the day off. They could call in sick for several days, take vacation time, or fabricate a family emergency. Some use the time to think; others update their resume and call recruiters or networking contacts.

Some VPs leave within weeks; others leave after several months. With time, some embrace their new role and remain with the company. Let the situation play out while offering the VP all the encouragement possible.

## Support

Letting an employee know their value and recognizing their unique talent goes a long way. Don't stop there. Back it up. If you really want them to organize new hire orientation or call exclusively on the largest customers, send them to a training course in that subject matter right away. No words from you will have as great an impact as that gesture. It demonstrates your continued investment in them.

# Danger zone

Be prepared for this during the initial conversation or weeks later. The current VP of sales will likely approach you with ideas for different titles. Most suggestions usually involve retaining the words "vice president."

They might request the title of vice president of new hire development or vice president of national accounts. These titles make the change appear more *lateral* in nature, versus a demotion.

Stay strong. Don't acquiesce to yet another title you don't want. Avoid putting yourself in the position of potentially having to take *another* title away. The label "vice president" carries certain implications. Agree only to a title you feel comfortable with. It should accurately reflect their duties and responsibilities at the company.

# The sales management position

In an ideal world, the current VP accepts the sales role without issue. You then promote one of the other reps to sales manager (or hire from the outside). But negotiating changes with the current VP occasionally proves difficult. It might take some time.

The rep you're considering for the sales management role might have ideas you hadn't considered. He could turn the position down.

The current VP wasn't really managing the reps. In reality, you've been operating without a sales manager all along. Don't rush into this. Spend the time necessary working out the details with the former VP. Then approach the other employee about the sales management position.

# Current staff

In most cases, I recommend speaking to the sales staff as a group. But this situation involves a demotion for a valued employee. Out of respect, meet with the reps individually. Relay a consistent message as you talk with each of them.

During these chats, emphasize the company's *future*—not the demotion of the current VP. Set the tone for growth and change. Talk about all the new initiatives taking place—both in the next few weeks and the next few years.

Just as you did when speaking with the VP, go over a little company history. Review the current setup through an organizational chart. Then show the future-based organizational chart. Don't use names, just titles.

From there, mention specifics. Tell the rep you've asked the current VP to take on a new role. Explain why. Say something like, "When I hired you, I asked Gina to help train you. She did a fantastic job. You benefitted from her mentoring. As we grow and bring on more new reps, we need to formalize new hire training. I can't think of anyone better qualified for new hire development."

Encourage questions and dialogue throughout the entire conversation. Give a timetable for all the changes taking place.

## Moving forward

Potentially awkward situations abound as reps enter into new roles. Sometimes deposed VPs gracefully relinquish the role initially, but turn toxic after a period of time.

In some companies, good manners prevail initially, then conflict bubbles up weeks later. Tense beginnings sometimes mellow into acceptance and reconciliation after a period of time. People's personalities change during times like these.

Avoid making predictions. No amount of pre-planning prevents all the bumps in the road during a reorganization of this magnitude. Deal with each situation as it arises.

## Hiring

Before making changes to the VP of sales position, you wrote new, future-oriented job descriptions and updated corresponding titles. When interviewing future applicants, share all of this information.

Going forward, don't allow new hires to dictate terms when it comes to titles. They might serve in a sales capacity with their current employer, but carry the title of marketing manager or customer relations specialist. They probably want to retain that title or have another one in mind altogether.

Tell them you understand different companies have different titles for reps. Reiterate that the title for the open position they're applying for is sales representative. Ask about their comfort level with the title. If they really balk, move on to other candidates.

## New hire orientation

Maximize the new hires' early weeks with the company by creating a sales toolkit to include information such as: introductory scripts, common objections, and proposal templates. This significantly accelerates the learning process for new sales reps.

If the former VP accepts a new hire training role, have them head up this project. Be sure she includes updated organizational charts and job descriptions. New reps get a look at future jobs they might aspire to, like sales manager.

## Leadership opportunities

Leaders make tough calls and initiate difficult conversations. The best look unemotionally and pragmatically at situations that no longer work for the company. After some serious thought, they put the necessary changes in place.

When the wrong person holds the VP of sales position, the other sales reps:

- Question your judgment.
- Show little regard for the chain of command.
- Feel stagnated in their career.
- See no room for advancement.
- Go to work for another company.

Reps have no respect for VPs with few qualifications for the job. For the overall good and future growth of your organization, put the right people in the right positions. As the company changes, adjust personnel accordingly.

## Summary checklist
### VP of sales review and checklist

- Clarify problem.
- Understand the role of VP of sales.
- Plan 3–5 years into the future:
  - Write job descriptions
  - Create organizational chart

- Consider new role(s) for the current VP of sales.
- Speak with the current VP of sales.
- Consider appropriate person for sales management role.
- Address sales staff.
- Provide targeted coaching or training.

# Resolution

Prior to the meeting, Carl listed Gina's potential objections to his new plan. He had spent the last day or so rehearsing responses. Carl prepared himself for anger or disbelief. As he explained the details of the reorganization, Gina just looked hurt. She didn't say a word. He had no plan for deafening silence and it threw him off.

In spite of this, he continued on bravely, "When I hired Pauline and Max, I asked you to train them. You did a fantastic job. I was very impressed. My plans include hiring two new reps in the next 18 months. Along with your sales duties, I was wondering if you'd consider being in charge of new hire orientation?"

Gina looked at him, shrugged her shoulders, and said, "I'll let you know. Is there anything else?"

For a week, she came into the office, politely said good morning to everyone, and then made her sales calls as always. She kept her distance from Pauline and Max. She and Carl spoke only when necessary.

During week two, she approached Carl about not only being in charge of new hire orientation, but writing a sales training manual. Her ideas included defining and formalizing the steps in the current sales process as well as creating scripts for voice and e-mail messages. She asked that her title be changed to director of new hire training.

Carl was relieved to see Gina back to her old self. He really believed no one was better qualified to write the new hire manual. However, the title she requested gave him pause. He didn't want to make another mistake in that area. Through the next 18 months, they would be adding only two new reps. Director of new hire training seemed over the top.

They negotiated. Gina agreed to the title of sales representative. On her business cards, under Sales Representative, the words New Hire Training Specialist would appear. That decided, they spoke more comfortably about his various decisions. Relations between all of them grew more cordial. During week three, Carl began to discuss the sales management position with Max.

Carl can't say for sure whether or not Gina will remain with the company. He doesn't know if reporting to Max will ever be comfortable for her. What he does know is that he made the right decision for the company. He feels confident the rest will work itself out.

# Chapter 15
# **High Base Salary**

Matt met Randy at a tradeshow where each of their employers had a booth. Matt was the sales manager for an "up and coming" company. Randy worked as a sales rep for their larger, well-known competitor. Matt introduced himself to other reps whenever he could. He felt more comfortable recruiting sales reps through networking, not ads or recruiters.

As they chatted during a break, Matt sensed Randy wasn't happy with his current employer. He mentioned issues like smaller territories and lower commissions. A new VP of sales had been hired, he added, and was putting all the reps through sales training. Randy didn't care for the methodology.

When Matt asked if he'd be interested in discussing the open sales position at his company, Randy said yes.

During the interview process, Randy asked for a high base salary—$150,000, higher than the typically $80–$85,000 Matt paid. Matt balked. Randy countered with talk about his solid contacts at national accounts, the revenue those accounts would generate, and the guaranteed income he was leaving behind. He mentioned his training, years of experience, and having to rebuild his pipeline if he joined Matt's company.

Randy produced all requested documentation: W2 forms, sales reports, and contest results. The information confirmed his sales and accomplishments. Matt went to bat with Patricia, his company's president, finally getting her to agree to the high base.

One year later, Matt stares at Randy in pure disbelief. Is this the same guy? Yes, he's selling, but just enough to justify his base salary. Seemingly completely content with low and sporadic commission checks, discussions about the lack of productivity go nowhere.

Patricia isn't happy with either one of them at this point. Matt bitterly regrets agreeing to Randy's demands. What does he do now?

---

### **Problem summary**

Sales rep
- Negotiated a high base salary
- Made promises about revenue goals based on
  - Experience
  - Contacts
  - Training
- Underperforming within his territory
- Content with base salary and minimal commission

Sales manager
- Regrets agreeing to the high base salary
- Embarrassed and let down by the rep's sales performance
- Confused by the lack of motivation
- Feels taken advantage of and stuck with the rep
- Experiences guilt regarding reps with lower bases

Managers dealing with this problem often feel angry, baffled, duped, and frustrated. Some wonder if anyone else has ever made this mistake. Believe me, they have. Managers get talked into salary arrangements like this again and again.

Initially, sales leaders in this situation make a lot of the right moves. They take the time to meet and recruit well-regarded reps from other companies. Putting together an attractive compensation package, they convince reps to work for their organization.

Take pride in your efforts. You meant for this to go well. Don't take all of the blame. Possibilities for this rep's underperformance include:

- Exaggerated track record of prior quota achievement.
- Overstated accomplishments.
- Lifestyle change, reducing money worries.
- Unexpected distractions outside of work.
- Poor fit between the rep and the company.

Managers need to consider that:

- When asked to produce documentation, reps show future employers *prior* reports. Their performance might have been spiraling down.
- Former top producers sometimes find themselves on probation or formal written warning with their current company. They need to find a job.
- Though they may have *earned* more money before, this might be the first time they've had a *base salary* this comfortable.
- Sometimes reps discover they can get along on a generous base salary just fine.

Whatever the reasons, you aren't permanently stuck in this situation. Step back from the turbulent emotions and begin fixing the situation. You can change it.

## Getting started

Research the salaries for sales representatives in similar industries on compensation-based Websites. Call colleagues in other areas of the country. Ask about their sales force compensation plans, including base salaries, commission, and bonuses. Take the geographic area and cost of living into consideration.

Create a chart to help you gather and organize the key facts:

| Company | Job Title | Base Salary | Commission | Quota | Location |
|---------|-----------|-------------|------------|-------|----------|
| Tell & Davidson | Sales Rep | $ 95,000 | $25k–$65K | $2.8 mil | Seattle |
| ALJ Associates | Account Mgr. | $ 105,000 | $35k–$75K | $3.2 mil | NYC |
| Rhodes Corp. | Sales Rep | $ 90,000 | $20k–$60K | $3.0 mil | St. Louis |

Understanding the pay range offered by other companies provides a standard to guide you in this process. The research shows an average base salary of about $95,000 and an average quota of $3 million.

Next, take a look at your own reps' salaries. Use another chart to organize their compensation information.

| Sales Rep | Title | Base Salary | Commission | Quota |
|-----------|-------|-------------|------------|-------|
| Tony | Sales Rep | $   80,000 | $30K–$60K | $2.4 mil |
| Alison | Sales Rep | $   75,000 | $30K–$60K | $2.3 mil |
| Chase | Sales Rep | $   83,000 | $30K–$60K | $2.3 mil |
| Randy | Sales Rep | $   150,000 | $40K–$79K | $3.0 mil |

Especially in a company that adds only one or two reps per year, managers lose track of who earns what in terms of a base salary.

## Gather the data

As I say throughout book, minimize negative feelings by equipping yourself with the facts. Forget about goals set and promises made. Review this rep's actual performance. Then speak with him about the situation.

Managers hiring top-performing reps away from a competitor often set aggressive goals. They do so in part to justify the base salary and because they believe the rep has that kind of potential.

Randy negotiated and agreed to a $3 million quota, an increase from last year of $1 million (50 percent) in the territory he will cover.

## Actual performance

Randy finished the year at $2,060,000 or 69 percent of quota—a modest increase of $60,000 and 3 percent more than the revenue achieved by the previous rep in the territory.

|  | Q1 | Q2 | Q3 | Q4 | Total |
|---|---|---|---|---|---|
| **Quota** | $ 750,000 | $ 750,000 | $ 750,000 | $ 750,000 | $ 3,000,000 |
| **Actual** | $ 480,000 | $ 520,000 | $ 495,000 | $ 565,000 | $ 2,060,000 |
| **Difference** | $ 270,000 | $ 230,000 | $ 255,000 | $ 185,000 | $ 940,000 |
| **% of Quota** | 64% | 69% | 66% | 75% | 69% |

## Major accounts

The five largest accounts in Randy's territory accounted for 75 percent of his sales. Due to his claims of strong contacts at each account, Randy's quota reflected an expected 50 percent increase in production from these accounts.

| Company | Last Year Sales | This Year Sales | Difference | % |
|---|---|---|---|---|
| **iStart** | $ 410,000 | $ 400,000 | $ (10,000) | 98% |
| **MLP Distribution** | $ 322,000 | $ 330,000 | $ 8,000 | 102% |
| **McClelland Corp.** | $ 286,000 | $ 295,000 | $ 9,000 | 103% |
| **Torman Foods** | $ 243,000 | $ 198,000 | $ (45,000) | 81% |
| **GoTrakkers** | $ 239,000 | $ 357,000 | $ 118,000 | 149% |
| **Total** | $ 1,500,000 | $ 1,580,000 | $ 80,000 | 105% |

Randy comes in at 70 percent of the major account quota for the year, realizing an $80,000 (5 percent) increase over the previous year's revenue.

## Consider other attributes

Revenue remains the key. But I advise sales leaders to evaluate additional areas of importance when thinking about this rep's performance, including:

- Product knowledge.
- Achievement of minimum productivity standards.
- Interactions with team members.
- Communications with employees in other departments.

## Findings

Gathering data and considering other factors allows you to compile an accurate picture of the high base salary rep. After looking at the numbers, some managers feel even angrier. Most express great disappointment.

This exercise, no matter how painful, gives you the confidence to move forward and make the needed changes.

### Create a plan

To solve the salary challenge, I advise sales leaders to make two changes at the same time:

- Standardize compensation for all sales reps.
- Reduce this rep's high base salary through a period of time.

## Compensation standardization

Large companies typically standardize pay for all positions, sometimes with adjustments to account for regional cost of living differences. Sales roles within the sales department might include: inside, field, government, education, and national account sales. Human resources and finance research competitive compensation plans, develop sales and compensation models, and create the compensation packages. Often, department leaders have no say in the matter.

List the positions within your sales department. Based on what you discovered as you researched pay ranges in your industry, put together a standard compensation plan for each one. For the position of sales representative, offer a base salary of $90,000 and commission between $40,000 and $65,000 against a typical quota of $2,500,000.

## Industry norms

Although Randy received a higher than normal base salary, he was hired as a field sales representative. He received no special title or account list. Your research places the base salary pay range for a salesperson in your industry at approximately $95,000 and the annual commission at $30,000–$70,000.

Based on your findings, recommend a base salary of $90,000 with annual commission of approximately $40,000–$65,000 as the standard for sales representatives working for your organization.

## Salary reduction

You offered this rep a compensation package to include a $150,000 base salary and commissions of more than $30,000. Even though it didn't work out as planned, managers need to acknowledge the commitment. I advise sales leaders in this situation to reduce the rep's annual salary during a three month period: month one ($135,000), month two ($120,000), and month three ($105,000).

By month four, the rep's base salary has been reduced to the standard compensation level of $90,000. The potential for commission/bonus remains the same.

## Present the plan to executives

Undoubtedly, you and your direct supervisor and/or human resources have spoken about this situation. It could be a source of major tension between the two of you. She might be questioning your recruiting and leadership abilities.

You hired this rep. You fought for the higher base salary. You had certain expectations from a revenue perspective. The situation has been a bust from beginning to end. Now make it right.

Present your plan for solving the problem. Give as objective an assessment as possible of the rep's overall performance. If possible, point out a few accomplishments. Take your share of the blame for the current state of their territory.

Consider any comments, critiques, or suggestions from your supervisor. Your supervisor may want to run the comp plan by finance. With both the compensation standardization and salary reduction plans finalized, prepare for a conversation with the rep.

---

Quick tip: Make sure to bring up the possibility of this rep quitting if his comp plan gets changed in any significant way. With a documented base salary of $150K, he may very well use this as a negotiating point with another company. Talk about a strategy for covering his accounts and replacing him if need be.

---

## Address the issue with the rep

My clients express surprise when I recommend focusing the discussion on the standardization of sales salaries, not about the rep's underperformance. The advice initially feels counterintuitive.

Concentrating on a lack of revenue generation, I explain, leads to unwinnable arguments. A sales manager says, "We sold almost $250,000 worth of product to Torman Foods last year. Since you took over the territory, they purchased less than $200,000."

The rep counters with statements about troubles with the new head of engineering at Torman and the unrealistic and demotivating 50-percent increase you expected (even if he agreed to it to justify the high base salary).

An argument starts. No one wins. Present the change as being about standardization. Use the nonperformance issue as *backup* and *support* for the decision.

Begin the discussion with a statement such as, "When you and I first met at the trade show, we discussed the company's plans for growth. You said it was one of the reasons you were interested in coming to work for us. Companies in growth mode need to control costs. I'm standardizing base pay and commission for the sales department. In field sales, this is the new compensation plan."

Allow the rep to review the plan. Get ready for what they have to say. Responses run the gamut, including:

- Disbelief.
- Outrage.
- Promises to improve.
- Asking for one more year.

Stay calm and focused. Reiterate, "As the company grows, we cannot have different people in the same department earning very different salaries. We need to standardize."

Repeat this as many times as you need to. Then move forward.

"We agreed to pay you a $150,000 base salary. I want to respect that. I've come up with a plan to gradually reduce your base pay. In month four, you'll be earning the standard $90,000 annually."

Review the chart with the rep. You never know what could happen next. Some reps accept the decision. They know the poor performance of the past year leaves little room for argument. Others fight to retain the base. If they insist on continuing the discussion, bring out the numbers.

Show them the original spreadsheets created for this discussion. Follow with a graph, presenting a strong case visually.

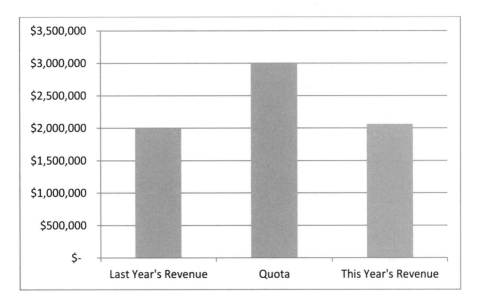

Then simply say, "I understand you're upset about the reduction in base pay. As a company, we need to standardize the compensation. Based on your performance, we cannot make an exception."

Don't engage in an argument. Keep repeating this.

## Setting future expectations

Enamored of the reps' background and experience, you set the bar too high. When things started going south, you didn't manage the situation as well as you might have. Anxious to get the job, the rep exaggerated accomplishments and made foolish promises. Even though your two companies were in the same industry, learning your product line could have proven more difficult than he had thought. Previous contacts didn't necessarily all greet him with open arms.

No matter what transpired during this last year, you wanted this to be a huge success for you, for the rep, and for the company. Let him know this. After everything settles down, set a time to meet again. Get to the heart of what went wrong. Together, come up with a plan to make this work.

Most importantly, customer by customer, revise the sales plan for his entire territory. Talk about corporate expectations. Ask about his revenue projections for each account. Understand the reasoning behind his estimates. Agree on the final number.

## Current staff

Word always gets around. The other reps probably know, or at least have an idea about, this rep's inflated base salary. You cannot discuss one employee's compensation with another. That information remains confidential for all employees.

In this case, the compensation issue affects the entire sales department. During a staff meeting, briefly review the company history. Talk about reps having different base salaries because the company added a new rep every year or two for a period of time.

Explain that corporate growth goes hand-in-hand with managing costs as well as offering standardized but competitive salaries. Review the new compensation plan with the group. Answer any questions. Let the staff know you'll be meeting with them one-on-one to discuss changes to their individual compensation plans, address concerns, and answer any questions.

## One-on-one discussions

Companies occasionally take corrective action by making adjustments to employees' compensation. These changes aren't universally popular. If your organization pays different sales reps different base salaries, standardizing represents a welcome raise for some and an unwanted pay cut for others. For those facing a significant reduction in their base, be sure to offer the option of reducing it during a period of three or four months.

For some, you might have to go through the exercise of running numbers for their territory or reviewing competitive salaries to make your point. To keep a good rep, put forth the effort. Hiring a replacement is costly and takes up much more of your time.

# Hiring

At some future point, you might have the opportunity to hire another superstar candidate. This could put you in the position of negotiating out of the pay range again.

Handle the process differently this time around. Before entering into serious talks with the candidate, involve your direct supervisor right away. Together:

- Establish the maximum salary offer.
- Agree on and set revenue quotas.
- Allow for ramp-up time with graduated goals.
- Set monthly and quarterly performance minimums.

During pre-employment discussions with the candidate:

- Negotiate specific accounts and territory.
- Request an account-by-account revenue estimate.
- Use revenue ranges, not specific numbers.

Most superstars worry about a loss of income while they build a new pipeline. Consider their point of view and future contributions to the company. Give some thought to offering a *temporary* higher base salary that gets decreased gradually during a three- or four-month period of time (depending on your average sales cycle).

To maximize their chances of success:

- Provide a comprehensive orientation to your organization.
- Meet with them regularly.
- Acknowledge and address any problems immediately.

Let them know you expect a hefty percentage of their income to come through bonuses or commission, not their base salary.

## Leadership opportunities

You saw the hiring of this sales rep as a coup for you and the company. With high expectations, you announced their arrival. But the rep didn't produce like you thought they would. You ignored early warning signs and made excuses:

- He's taking a while to get up to speed.
- Big differences exist between the two companies' product lines.
- His numbers will start to climb soon.

The other salespeople (and employees in other departments too) undoubtedly know this much-heralded superstar hasn't lived up to expectations. Some sales reps might resent the new hire, viewing him with a mixture of jealousy and contempt.

Businesspeople make mistakes—hiring and otherwise. Whole books, case studies, newspaper columns, Websites, and blogs get devoted to the subject. You made several slip-ups when hiring this individual. If you had to do it over again, you would handle the whole situation differently. You learned from the experience. That means professional growth.

The reps watch and wait to see how you address this problem. You're under the microscope. Earn everyone's respect by stepping up, admitting some culpability, and addressing the issue.

## Summary checklist
### High base salary review and checklist

- Clarify problem.
- Research industry compensation norms.
    - Standardize the compensation plans for different sales positions

- Document salesperson's performance to date.
- Adjust the rep's base salary.
- Share plan with direct supervisor.
- Speak with the underperforming rep.
- Revisit and revise the sales plan.

# Resolution

Red-faced and angry, Randy yells at Matt, "Standardize base salaries! What a joke. You hired me because you said you were tired of finishing second or third to the competition. It's more like fourth or fifth. All the buyers say the same thing: We need that second valve to compete. And guess what—we don't have it."

After that speech, Randy leaves Matt's office, not to be heard from for the rest of the day. Late that afternoon, he calls Matt to apologize for storming out. He asks if Matt will meet with him after work. Matt says yes.

While waiting for Randy, Matt thinks things over. He gave Randy overly ambitious sales goals. As Randy struggled, Matt panicked but acted passively. He didn't meet with him regularly or put up much of a fight when Randy refused help. Instead, he assumed Randy would figure it all out and save the day. It showed naïveté and poor judgment on his part.

He takes issue with Randy's comment about the second valve. In his experience, with most sales that second valve isn't a deal breaker. For many companies, it's a "nice to have," not a "must have." That's an excuse and lack of salesmanship on Randy's part.

Randy walks into Matt's office, flashing a peace sign. They start talking.

Randy admits he thought moving from the largest player to an up-and-coming competitor would be much easier. The pricing structure really confused him at first. He handled the customers' objection about the second valve like a rookie salesperson. Embarrassed about his performance, he rejected any offers of help. He, too, thought the situation would turn around.

When he asks for another year on the higher base salary, Matt says no. Randy seems disappointed, but resigned to the situation.

Randy agrees to work with Matt on a new sales plan. Now that he's been in the territory for a year, he has a better idea of the revenue potential. Randy plans to meet with product development to gain a greater understanding of the technology and with finance to review pricing. He and Matt set up a weekly meeting.

Both acknowledge wanting this situation to work. Randy lost interest in remaining with his former employer when they cut territories and commission. His desire to work for a smaller, growth-oriented company was genuine. Matt was thrilled to hire an experienced, high-profile rep like Randy. They agree to work together to make this next year successful.

# Index

# About the Author

Suzanne Paling is a recognized leader in sales management. With more than 25 years of experience in field and inside sales, sales management, and sales management consulting and coaching, she has helped more than 55 companies improve their sales performance and processes. Clients include product and service firms in the manufacturing, software, publishing, distribution, medical, and construction industries. Docurated has selected Suzanne's blog as one of their "Top 50 Sales Management Blogs." She writes for *Entrepreneur* magazine and *American Business Magazine*, and publishes a monthly newsletter. Suzanne's work with one of her clients, an ambulance service, was profiled in the *New York Times* Small Business column. Suzanne is the author of the award-winning book *The Accidental Sales Manager*, a finalist for a Best Books 2010 Award from *USA Book News*.

For more than 15 years, Sales Management Services has provided practical advice to company presidents, owners, entrepreneurs, and business executives seeking to increase revenue by improving their sales organization's performance. Among its clients are product and service firms in manufacturing, software, construction, medical, telecommunications, recruiting, delivery, and distribution.

## Sales Management Services provides expert assistance in areas including:

- Management (organization and processes)
- Coaching (sales management)
- Assessments
- Hiring process
- Planning
- Operations

## For each new project, Sales Management Services works closely with the client to:

- Identify top objectives for your sales organization
- Determine path to achieving objectives
- Evaluate skills of the sales force
- Define key success criteria for ideal salesperson
- Institute a hiring procedure
- Set productivity standards
- Develop or improve sales reporting system
- Create/implement performance review process
- Promote a culture of accountability and success

## Sales Management Coaching

Sales Management Services provides one-on-one sales management coaching advice to CEOs, presidents, and sales executives (VPs, directors, and managers) seeking to increase revenue by improving their sales organization's performance.

# Along with the objectives above, for each coaching project Sales Management Services works closely with the executive (sales leader) to:

- Create a structure and process for managing
- Determine leadership strengths/challenges
- Identify management style
- Review pipeline and forecast reports
- Establish individual rep and department goals

## Speaking engagements

Looking for a way to inspire the sales executives in your organization? Suzanne Paling talks to sales management groups about a variety of sales management related topics including: hiring, motivating, improving staff sales skills, and goal setting. Attendees receive practical, realistic advice and tips that they are able to start using immediately after the presentation.

## Newsletter

*Sales Management Tips* addresses the sales management concerns and questions of a broad based, domestic, and foreign small business readership. We provide guidance for addressing problems within the sales organization, share relevant survey results, and recommend books and magazines for readers seeking more extensive information on a particular topic.

Sign up for the newsletter at *www.salesmanagementservices.com.*

Suzanne Paling

Sales Management Services

Suzanne.Paling@SalesManagementServices.com

*www.salesmanagementservices.com*

LinkedIn: *www.linkedin.com/in/suzannepaling*

Twitter: @SuzannePaling